Millennial Apprentices: The Next Revolution In Freemasonry

Samuel Friedman

Sam Friedman
16 Kerry Hill
Fairport NY 14450

Publisher's Cataloging-in-Publication data:

Friedman, Samuel.
Millennial Apprentices: The Next Revolution In Freemasonry / Sam Friedman
p. cm.
ISBN 978-0-9966528-0-3
1. Freemasonry —History —Current Events. 2. Millennial Generation.

First Edition
14 13 12 11 10 / 10 9 8 7 6 5 4 3 2 1

To my mother, father, brother and Erica.
I love you all.

Table of Contents

Acknowledgements

Though he may not know it, this book was directly inspired by my brother Jake. Writing a book was always something I dreamed of, but I assumed I did not have the talent required to actually produce one, therefore it would be a dream forever out of my reach. Jake showed me the influential TED talk given by Prof. Larry Smith entitled *Why You Will Fail to Have a Great Career*. Though this book has nothing to do with my career goals, Professor Smith's lecture resonated with me. I avoided writing because I was afraid. I was afraid of embarrassment and afraid of rejection. This book is the physical manifestation of me conquering that fear, and for that I am eternally grateful to Jake for inspiring me with that video.

I have many reasons to be grateful for my family. I am grateful that my father brought me into the Fraternity, grateful that he is always willing to share his wealth of experience and knowledge, and grateful that he is a wonderful and supporting father.

My mother, who acted as my first editor, was often my first phone call after a new idea for a chapter or section popped into my head. She has been an ever present and steady force in my life. The completing of this book is as much a testament to her tenacity as to mine.

Lois Taubman professionally edited my work. Her advice was invaluable and she steered me clear of several rookie pitfalls.

To the dozens of Brothers in several countries who provided invaluable support, information and time to me and this project. You are a testament to the universality of this Fraternity and your example has been an inspiration to me.

And lastly, to my longtime companion, Erica. Who has endured the idiosyncrasies of my personality longer than any person should, for that I love you and I always will.

INTRODUCTION

WHY WOULD A YOUNG MAN JOIN THE world's oldest fraternity? In hindsight this is a question I should have asked myself while sitting in the Chamber of Reflection just outside the door of my mother Lodge. As many Masons know, the Chamber of Reflection is a space set aside for candidates to contemplate their own unique motivations for joining Freemasonry. Candidates are required to spend time in the Chamber before completing all three Degrees required to become a Master Mason. Some candidates use their time in the Chamber for meditation; others see it as a chance to pray to whatever deity in which they believe. Some have no idea what the Chamber is because they receive little or no direction about how to use it.

The other men and I who were raised in December 2012 chose our own path, telling lewd jokes so loudly we were told to settle down on more than one occasion. Perhaps that is regrettable.

We all could have benefited from asking ourselves why young men such as we would consider joining Freemasonry. One man was a twenty-eight-year-old real estate appraiser at his father's company. Another man, was a forty-one-year-old lawyer and professor at a State University. Another was a thirty-six-year-old sales executive for a nationwide insurance company. And the final member of my class was a twenty-seven-year-old aspiring artist, teaching pottery classes on the side while he developed his career. As for me, at the time, I was a junior at the State University. We all had reasons for joining Freemasonry. Mine was relatively straightforward.

It's in my blood.

My family's association with Freemasonry started with my great uncle, Sam Brotman. A pharmacist and part-time bowling-alley operator, Sam hailed from the Lower East Side of Manhattan. In his day, the Lower East Side was a predominantly Jewish neighborhood that was home to the teeming tenements depicted in such films as *Hester Street* and *The Godfather*.

Why Sam joined Freemasonry has unfortunately been lost in the sands of time, but his membership was very important to him. His three brothers were also members. Sam belonged to the Fraternity for thirty-seven years and served as Master of his Lodge, Golden Rule #770, which met on Lenox Avenue in Harlem.[1] As important as Masonry was to Sam, his extended family was never aware of his membership. This group included his nephew and surrogate son, my father.

My father had never thought of joining Freemasonry until one cold day in 1984. Sam, seventy-seven years old at the time, called to tell my father some terrible news. He had been diagnosed with pancreatic cancer. The doctors predicted that he had only a year left to live, and that was the most positive prognosis they had to offer. My father, flabbergasted by the news, asked what he could do for Sam in his final days. Sam had only one request of my father, he wanted him to join the Fraternity he loved so dearly.

This request took my father completely by surprise. This was something very different from the usual deathbed request. He had vaguely heard of the Freemasons but never knew that his Uncle Sam was a member. He also had no idea how one would go about joining them.

There was no phone number listed in the Yellow Pages, nor were there any billboards or television ads, and in 1984 the Internet was not yet available, so surfing for his local Lodge on the net was not an option either. My father was at a complete loss as to how to fulfill his beloved uncle's final request.

In total desperation he turned to a co-worker of his who happened to sport the last name of Mason, thinking somebody with that last name might know something about the Freemasons. Luckily for him, his co-worker actually happened to be a Freemason and was able to introduce him to his fellow Brothers and enter my father into the initiation process.

Thus, my father was raised at Ancient Craft Lodge #943 on June 3, 1985. His Uncle Sam was in attendance for all three of his Degrees.

Exactly one hundred days later, Uncle Sam passed away, finally succumbing to his disease. My father had only joined Freemasonry to honor his dying uncle. When he first embarked on his Masonic journey he had assumed that after his uncle passed, he would quietly not renew his membership. But between entering Ancient Craft Lodge as an entered apprentice and his raising as a Master Mason, my father had discovered a spiritual brotherhood that reinforced the core principles that he believed in strongly: brotherhood, philanthropy, and truth. He was determined to live a Masonic life. He took to this new path with passion and zeal. My father quickly moved through the leadership positions of his Lodge. His Lodge was in dire condition, marked by revolving door leadership. He became Master in less than four years. He went on to hold both District and Statewide office.

I was involved with all of these positions and responsibilities very intimately, even at a very young age. An application was filled out for me on my first birthday and I was made an honorary Mason that day.

That application has hung on the wall of my childhood bedroom for the past twenty-four years. I helped set up the Lodge room on meeting nights, placing the symbolic jewels and aprons of the different officers on their appropriate chairs when my father was secretary. And to complete the story, even my first kiss took place in the basement of a Shrine center! As the years passed, Ancient Craft merged with several Lodges, eventually adopting the moniker ERAC, reflecting all of the Lodges that merged to form it. ERAC Lodge became my mother Lodge. So when I say ERAC is my mother Lodge I mean that quite literally. ERAC has been a part of my life since the day I was born.

In the year 2000, my father was elected to the Grand Line as Junior Grand Warden of the State of New York. He served his Grand Master, Carl Smith. Grand Master Smith's unique directive for Grand Line officers was to connect rural Lodges to Grand Lodge in a manner not done in modern times. This meant that the Grand Line officers traveled the length and breadth of New York State visiting Lodges so remote that even local law enforcement were sometimes befuddled as to their exact location. I remember my father going on these long trips into the hinterland of New York State. I never quite understood why, but I assumed it must have been something important for him to leave us so often.

After many Chairmanships and honors, my father achieved his Masonic dream of becoming Chairman of the Custodians of the Work. For those of you who are unfamiliar with what the Custodians do, they are a group of preeminent Masonic scholars who have two responsibilities: They interpret and issue rulings on Masonic Ritual controversies brought to them by the various Lodges of their constituency; and they preserve and propagate the Masonic Ritual among that same constituency.

My father was Chairman of the Custodians when I turned 21. This meant I was finally eligible to join a Masonic Lodge in New York State. Knowing this, my father sat me down and explained that I should not feel obligated to join a Lodge. Something like this should be my decision, and I should not feel pressured by any outside influence. The truth is I never once considered abstaining from Freemasonry. The same can be said for my younger brother, who also shared a similar experience of interaction with the Lodge as a child. As I said, Freemasonry was just "in my blood."

It is at this point, we return to the Chamber of Reflection on the night of my First Degree. Instead of contemplating all of this: my childhood journey, my coming of age, and my pride in my father and myself, I was too busy discussing my favorite Canadian trailer park comedy with the other members of my class.

In this somewhat cavalier way, I entered my Masonic journey. I really had no expectations for the Fraternity. I knew what it meant to my father, but I had never considered what I wanted from the Craft. As I explored the options my Lodge offered, I discovered things that I liked and things I disliked. Overall, I realized that, for me, the experience was lacking.

Our Lodge room closely resembles an airport hotel's conference room. It is a multi-purpose room that hosts all kinds of events and not just Lodge meetings. The main Lodge room is massive and can hold up to two hundred people, so even on a night when we have a stellar turnout, the room always manages to feel empty. While there are interesting things on the wall, even that space is multi-purpose. The Chamber of Reflection is no better. Despite its imposing name, it really is an adjoining unadorned conference room, not unlike anything you would find in a second rate office building anywhere in the country.

Our educational opportunities are mostly spent talking about Masonic history, and how great the organization used to be. Our Ritual work is crisp, but seems more geared to a self-perpetuating cycle of membership. Much of our Trestleboard is dedicated to either attracting or initiating new men into the Lodge. Meanwhile, these new men, who have been entering our front door, have increasingly been feeling let down and disappointed by their Masonic experience, and leaving by the back door.

To be clear, ERAC Lodge is in no way a failing lodge. In fact, ERAC is the premier Lodge in our district, full of enthusiastic and committed Brothers who have created a healthy reputation both locally and throughout the state. My criticisms are not a reflection on the Brothers of my Lodge, rather they are a reflection on the general state of the modern Fraternity. In my opinion, this makes those criticisms all the more damning, as Brothers from Honolulu to Maine can, and have, shared similar stories.

While talk of a membership problem is ubiquitous in modern Masonic discourse, the reality is that many Lodges do not have an issue attracting new men into the Fraternity. Rather, they have a retention problem. In the years since I joined ERAC, the Lodge has initiated almost six new Brothers a year!

Yet, the number of men actually attending Lodge meetings has remained relatively static. Although we derive active members from each class, our retention rate still suffers.

We are in the marketplace of ideas and we compete for people's time and loyalties. It became increasingly clear to me that Freemasonry was failing to initiate Brothers who became active in the Craft, especially with members of my own generation, the millennials.

While I was aware that my family connection led me on the path to Freemasonry, I couldn't help but wonder about the motivations of my fellow travelers. What would compel other young men, with so much else competing for their time and attention, to join a Masonic Lodge in the second millennium? What was the appeal? My curiosity led me to start asking around. In fact, I even created a brief survey that allowed millennial Brothers from around the country and the world to voice their opinions.

In asking the question, I found that the reasons for joining the Fraternity are as numerous and unique as its members.[2] Several themes that I heard frequently were: the search for spiritual fulfillment, a desire for fraternal bonding and universal brotherhood, becoming involved in their communities through charity, or because they were curious to be a part of something with a long and somewhat "secret" history. Freemasonry can be all of these things. Why was it not working as well as it could?

James, a young Brother who joined the Masons at the same time I did, joined the Lodge looking to connect to like-minded individuals while learning about himself in a sacred space that was unique in this "age of shallowness and online interaction." Another Mason in his early twenties, from central Kansas, joined Freemasonry to experience the spiritual esoterica the Craft has to offer a willing seeker. When asked why he joined Freemasonry, his laconic response was simply, "to explore the unknown."

Another young Mason from Ohio had been interested in Freemasonry since he was a child, professing, "I thought that Masons were the intellectuals who fought the good fight, trying to make the world a better place. I thought they were clever and hid secret meanings all around and looked at the world deeper than the average individual."

With expectations like this it is easy to see why so many young men join Lodges and then quietly demit their memberships. Most young men believe they are joining something ancient and elite and often what they discover is far more mundane than what they had hoped. I experienced many of the same frustrations and disappointments as many younger Brothers do.

So why did I not just demit, as so many do? A lot of this comes down to my family connection. I love my father and I love spending time with him. In a natural way, Freemasonry offered another avenue where I could bond with him. But I also sensed there was something more to Freemasonry than I had been experiencing in my Lodge.

So, like many others before me, including my father, I began to read, research, and talk to as many different Brothers from as many jurisdictions as I could.

In this process I discovered Observant Masonry.

Observant Masonry has managed to combine older traditions and practices with a modern interpretation of Freemasonry. Its umbrella organization, the Masonic Restoration Foundation (MRF), perceives its mission as the following:

"Young men tend to perceive Freemasonry as a venue for truth seeking, a vehicle for self-improvement and philosophical development; the discovery of one's inner potential. Our new brothers know what they want from a fraternity and have high expectations that their Lodge will meet their needs as men."

"As North American Freemasonry faces some of the most important challenges in its history, the MRF stands to ensure a sense of purpose and identity for the Craft."[3]

Intrigued and encouraged by this, I began to visit Observant Lodges. I was thoroughly impressed by the notion that a Lodge could actually be a sacred space, and perceived as such by the demeanor of its Brothers.

Observant Lodges can now be found in over twenty-five states and four Canadian provinces totaling close to fifty different Lodges. Even though I was becoming convinced the Observance Movement was a powerful reclamation of Masonry's original purpose and greatness, I also came to believe that the Observance Movement was only a partial reclamation of our traditional mission, and that more work was required.

I began to notice that while Observant Lodges had seemingly solved many of modern Masonry's ills, other troubles stubbornly persisted. Brother Robert Herd, a notable author, an advocate for Observant practices and founder of the *Living Stones Magazine*, offered an interesting quote on the subject in a podcast in 2015. When asked what the biggest challenges were in creating the *Living Stones Magazine* he answered:

"Fresh content..... Masonry only has so many symbols and you can only talk about them so many times.... and you can only read so many articles about George Washington."[4]

Upon further inspection I discovered that even at some of the most prestigious Observance Lodges in the country, those Brothers still devote much of their Trestleboard toward education in Masonic history.

Have you ever wondered why our ancient brethren were so busy making history and yet we are so busy only reading it?

There were several moments throughout time when young men from cities, towns, and villages all over the Western world flocked into Lodges to experience what the Craft had to offer. Some of these men would later go on to be among the most influential revolutionaries the world had ever seen. These Masons made history. These include the Marquis de Lafayette, John Hancock, John Paul Jones, José De San Martin, Benjamin Franklin, Simón Bolívar, Paul Revere, George Washington, and all the other familiar names we have heard so many times when other brethren are reading the roles of famous Freemasons. Many of them joined as young men. Washington was raised when he was twenty-one, Franklin at age twenty-five. The famous South American revolutionaries Bolívar and De San Martin were raised when the latter was thirty and the former was twenty. When the Marquis was raised is still a historical mystery, though a longstanding tradition states that he was raised at a military Lodge in Morristown, New Jersey when he was twenty-one. In the more recent past, Harry Truman joined when he was twenty-five, and Franklin Roosevelt joined when he was slightly older at age twenty-nine.

What attracted these young men of such passion, vigor and intelligence to Freemasonry? No need to paraphrase, they can tell us in their own words. Harry Truman believed:

"We represent a fraternity which believes in justice and truth and honorable action in your community. Men who are endeavoring to be better citizens and to make a great country greater." [5]

In a speech to the Lodge at the raising of his son, Franklin Roosevelt stated that Masonry acted:

"As a leaven for a better society and better citizenship" [6]

George Washington declared that the object of Masonry is:

"To promote the happiness of the human race." [7]

Theodore Roosevelt, raised when he was forty-three, said that:

"One of the things that attracted me so greatly to Masonry.... was that it really did live up to what we, as a government, are pledged to do, of treating each man on his merits as a man." [8]

What do all these statements have in common? These men believed that Freemasonry stood for a very specific set of ideals. These men recognized that Masonry stood for egalitarianism, democracy, freedom of thought and conscience, religious and racial tolerance and the universalism of all men under "The Great Architect of the Universe."

At the time many of these men were joining Freemasonry, these ideas were not only unpopular, but at times downright dangerous to voice.

The idea that men of all ranks, races and religions could dwell together in harmony was a bold and radical one. It countered much of Western scientific knowledge, political theory and religious theology that had been firmly established for over a millennia.

Meeting an observant Mason in eighteenth century America was as jarring to the sensibilities of the average citizen as meeting a fanatical anarchist or communist in the twenty-first century. In that context, it's easy to view Freemasonry as a reformist revolutionary organization. These young revolutionaries needed safe areas to meet like-minded peers and develop their ideas of equality and freedom. What better place than a Lodge guarded from "cowans and eavesdroppers?"

As Brother Richard Kidwell wrote in his controversial 1982 Short Talk Bulletin entitled, *Freemasonry: The Sleeping Giant.*

"They were inspired with the realization that Masonry is morality in action, and that their obligations at the altar of Freemasonry were sacred promises that required appropriate action. They were committed to a pursuit of excellence embodied in the teaching of the Fraternity. The urge for casting off bonds of oppression, for seeking equal rights for all, and for demanding the intellectual, moral, and spiritual freedom of the individual has always characterized Masons, not only in this country but also in others. Witness the great Masons around the world--Benito Juarez in Mexico, Simon Bolivar in South America, Jose Rizal in the Philippine Islands, for example. Wherever the need for reasserting the doctrine of right and freedom has emerged, Masons have taken a leading role in the quest for intellectual and moral liberty."[9]

I have always been taught that politics has no business in Freemasonry and that has always been espoused since the birth of the Fraternity. *The Ancient Charges*, Freemasonry's oldest rules and regulations, set this precedent by establishing that political conversations were inappropriate in Lodges because, "they have never yet conduced to the welfare of the Lodge." Those learned Brothers were partially correct. It should be noted, however, that often the word "politics" is used as an umbrella term. The true definition of the word "politics" is groups or individuals engaged in activities associated with either governing a country, or entering into a debate with the *hope* of achieving the power to govern.

At no point in our history has a Lodge or Grand Lodge ever attempted to govern a nation or engage in a debate with the hope of achieving power. Rather, Lodges, through Masonic philosophy, inspired men all over the world toward individual advocacy in their communities. This was not only tolerated, but encouraged by the Masonic culture of the time. So much so that a respected historian of the American Revolution declared,

"The fraternity played a key role in helping Americans remake their social order, shaping and symbolizing the transition from the aristocratic hierarchy of the eighteenth century to the democratic individualism of the nineteenth." [10]

Gradually this changed over time. In the modern day, even a whiff of espousing these values outside of the Lodge, as a Mason, is met with near hysteria.

This is not the case in other parts of the world.

I recently had the experience of traveling to the nation of Lebanon and visiting with several of the brethren there. Frequently and secretly meeting only blocks away from Hezbollah militants and defying an eighteenth century Fatwa, Lebanese Brothers risk being ostracized to attend Lodge. In a land racked with religious sectarian violence, the Masonic emphasis on tolerance, egalitarianism and democracy inspires these men to promote these ideas throughout their communities in the hope of ending the violence. Lebanese Brothers epitomize Joseph Fort Newton's belief that Freemasonry should act as a:

"Ministry to the individual, and through the individual to society and the state" [11]

As I was discovering the history of this change, I simultaneously began researching the generation of American males born after 1980, my generation, colloquially known as the millennials. Like previous generations before them, the millennials possess unique motivations, aspirations, and characteristics that differentiate their worldview and conception of themselves from other generational groups. The millennials recently have surpassed the baby boomers as the largest generation in American history, over seventy-five million strong in 2015 and expected to reach eighty-five million in 2036. The rise of this generation marks another turning point in American social culture and puts modern Freemasonry at a crossroads.

The millennial generation possesses many unique characteristics that may make Freemasonry a very attractive organization to them. So much so, that I believe we are on the verge of a renaissance of Freemasonry on this continent. But this great revival will not happen organically. Radical and active restoration is needed.

The Observance Movement has gone a long way toward this radical change, and has in turn attracted many newer and younger members to its ranks. But I believe the work is not yet complete. I must admit I am standing on the shoulders of the more learned Brothers who have come before me. The following set of ideas and actions should be used in conjunction with the tested values that have congregated under the "Observance" mantle.

I envision this philosophy as a mere extension of that tradition. Whether the elder statesmen of that philosophical branch of the Fraternity choose to accept it, I humbly leave it to them.

In two recent articles, Robert Davis, a highly respected modern Masonic author and thinker wrote,

"The existence of an active traditional Freemasonry in a democratic society is the best guarantee and assurance of genuine spiritual and civic freedom." [12]

If this is true, now is surely the time to prove it. Davis also declared,

"I have struggled agonizingly long over our institution's inertness to collectively put into practice what we preach. The biggest weakness of our order is that we have no way of organizing our strengths to collectively improve society in the name of Masonry." [13]

In this volume, I propose to show that this weakness is relatively modern and that our ancient brethren can provide us a blueprint to follow that will allow us to collectively organize our strengths to improve society as a whole.

Many of these ideas are not revolutionary. Almost all of them have been practiced before by our past brethren. But I believe our clarion call as Masons should be to task our brethren with the following mission.

Wherever men do not meet on the level that is where we should be laboring in the metaphorical stone quarries. Let every Lodge become a beacon in the community for learning. Let every Lodge inspire its members to individual advocacy work. If enough men are inspired to change the world, you will eventually have the beginnings of a revolution.

The Masonic scholar, William Grimshaw, once wrote that Masonry:

"Places man in harmony with all that is true and good, enlarging his powers for usefulness in every vocation, station, position or condition in life." [14]

Let us use this enlarged stature to change the world Brothers! That is a reason to come to Lodge, and that is a message millennials can rally around.

Before I get into specific proposals, which I hope will operationalize these grandiose words for individual Lodges, I would invite older Brothers to take the time to understand what makes millennials tick, to begin to understand what our motivations are and how Freemasonry could possibly fit into our lives. The goal of this book is to both educate and advocate. I wish to:

- Educate older Brothers about how millennials view the world and what expectations they bring to the Craft;
- Understand the experiences millennials hope to have in the Fraternity, and then to advocate for a removal of the artificial barriers that have been raised against Masons espousing their philosophical tenets to the greater society that surrounds them.

I will begin in the past, as I believe any worthwhile work does. For without studying the historical context of a problem, how can a proper diagnosis and remedy be recommended? As we will see, Freemasonry, for much of its history, was an important organization that contributed both the philosophical pillars western civilization currently stands on, and the men who were willing to fight and die for those same beliefs.

WHENCE CAME YOU

MUCH INK HAS BEEN DEVOTED TO THE illustrious history of the Craft. Brothers much more qualified than I have already written many articles, blogs, books, lectures, and brochures detailing the story of the Fraternity. In fact, so much has already been written on this topic, I actually hesitated to comment on it.

The sad fact is that modern Freemasonry has a bit of a fetish for Masonic history. When Lodges try to incorporate "Masonic Education" into their Trestleboards, the term is often really a euphemism for a Masonic history lecture. There is certainly a place for this. I am a firm proponent of analyzing the past, and I hope most Lodges have dedicated at least a few programs a year to this worthy endeavor. Unfortunately we have gone overboard. When we are constantly looking backward, we often fail to move forward.

Thomas Jefferson once remarked, *"I like the dreams of the future better than the history of the past."* [15]

I believe many of the men who joined this Fraternity in the past would agree with Mr. Jefferson, and they instilled this optimism into the Fraternity. Therefore, in an attempt to practice what I preach, this chapter will mark the end of the American Masonic history lecture. In subsequent chapters, I will turn to the Masonic present and more importantly the Masonic future.

Most Masonic scholars believe that the true origins of Freemasonry have been lost to time. There are many theories, but nothing substantial. The Masonic origin story is vague and has changed drastically over the years. James Anderson, the seventeenth century Scottish author of *The Ancient Constitutions of the Freemasons*, claimed that Freemasonry was so ancient that it existed in the world before the Great Flood of Noah. Anderson claimed that Noah himself was a Mason and through him and his three sons, Japheth, Shem, and Ham, Freemasonry was transmitted safely through the Great Flood and into the New World. According to Anderson, almost every major character of the Bible was trained in the Masonic arts. Anderson gives Moses the title General Master Mason. He postulates the Masonic arts spread through the Israelites to the land of Israel and eventually to Jerusalem, a small settlement in the Judean hills governing a few pastoral villages in its immediate vicinity. It wasn't until King David, the legendary slayer of Goliath, united the various Israelite tribes into the Kingdom of Israel, that Jerusalem became the political and spiritual capitol of the Jewish people.

The modern origin story of Freemasonry is set during the reign of David's son, King Solomon. Solomon was known for his wisdom and just decisions when dealing with his subjects. Solomon was tasked by God to build a splendid building to house the Ark of the Covenant, the vessel in which the original Ten Commandments were housed. Solomon spread this message to the other monarchs of the land. Hiram, the King of Tyre in Phoenicia, located in modern day Lebanon, was an old ally of Solomon's father David. Hiram offered his kingdom's expertise, and the two nations began a joint effort to build the temple. Phoenicia was home to magnificent forests of cedar trees, known throughout the ancient world as the best materials for building ships and other structures made of wood. They were extremely valuable, therefore, greatly prized throughout the near east.

King Hiram's subjects floated timber down the Mediterranean coast to the Israelites and provided thousands of laborers. Most significant to the history of Freemasonry, King Hiram sent one of his most trusted servants to be the chief architect of the temple. His name was Hiram Abiff. Hiram Abiff was the perfect candidate for this job for a variety of reasons. He straddled the cultural divide that had long separated the Israelites and Phoenicians. His father hailed from Tyre, while his mother was an Israelite belonging to either the tribe of Dan or Naphtali. Both tribes were located in the far north of Israel and had a long history of trade and communication with the Phoenician cities and villages just over the hills from their traditional lands. In addition to his cultural bona fides, Hiram also was a highly skilled Operative Mason. The Bible goes into great detail about the construction of the temple that Hiram oversaw, including Hiram's own personal skills. As the Book of Kings in the Old Testament tells us,

"Hiram he was filled with wisdom, and understanding, and cunning to work all works in brass. And he came to King Solomon, and wrought all his work. And he set up the pillars in the porch of the temple: and he set up the right pillar, and called the name thereof Jachin: and he set up the left pillar, and called the name thereof Boaz. And upon the top of the pillars was lily work: so was the work of the pillars finished. And Hiram made the lavers, and the shovels, and the basins. So Hiram made an end of doing all the work that he made King Solomon for the house of the LORD. The two pillars, and the two bowls of the chapiters that were on the top of the two pillars; and the two networks, to cover the two bowls of the chapiters which were upon the top of the pillars; And four hundred pomegranates for the two networks, even two rows of pomegranates for one network, to cover the two bowls of the chapiters that were upon the pillars; And the ten bases, and ten lavers on the bases; And one sea, and twelve oxen under the sea; And the pots, and the shovels, and the basins: and all these vessels, which Hiram made to King Solomon for the house of the LORD, were of bright brass. In the plain of Jordan did the king cast them, in the clay

ground between Succoth and Zarthan." [16]

The Bible says that over 113,000 workers were levied to provide the necessary manpower. These men hailed from Byblos, Tyre and all twelve tribes of Israel. Thirty thousand men were employed as log cutters in Lebanon, scything immense cedar trees and floating them down the Mediterranean Sea to the port of Jaffa, where they were transported overland to Jerusalem. Eighty thousand men were employed cutting stone in the Judean hills, and three thousand men were employed as managers and organizers of this immense workforce. To adequately organize and coordinate a multinational workforce of this size and geographical distance would have been an immense project, and Hiram would have to have been a tolerant, organized, and judicious executive.

According to the Masonic origin story, as the temple neared completion, three workmen, and brothers from Tyre, confronted Hiram Abiff and demanded the secrets of his craft which would allow them material prosperity and prestige unheard of to an amateur stonemason or farmer. This knowledge was only to be shared among Hiram and the two kings who oversaw his work. This information was so secret that the three executives made a pact that the secret knowledge would only be uttered when all three were present and accounted for.

After this confrontation, in a legendary act of loyalty and integrity, Hiram refused and was subsequently murdered. The three ruffians then fled Jerusalem hoping to escape the realm to safety. King Hiram of Tyre and King Solomon dispatched their army of craftsmen in every direction in pursuit of the ruffians. Upon their capture, King Solomon ordered their execution in retribution for the murder of such an upright and honorable man. Due to the pact sworn by the three men, Hiram's death essentially doomed any hope of transmitting his knowledge. Freemasonry, whose symbols and rituals are said to descend directly from King Solomon and his craftsmen, labors to retrieve this knowledge and carry on the memory of the slain Hiram.

The temple was eventually completed without Hiram Abiff and was widely known throughout history as one of the most ornate and holy buildings ever constructed. The temple served as the most holy Jewish site for 410 years until the Babylonian king, Nebuchadnezzar, leveled it to the ground after his successful siege of Jerusalem in 587 B.C.

Most modern Masons understand that this story should be taken as an allegory, not a real historical account. And while the building of King Solomon's Temple is shrouded in lore and myth, the medieval European stone guilds from which Freemasonry most likely sprang are much more intimately understood.

Most citizens of the medieval world were indentured farmers in service to a liege lord; this population became known as serfs. This feudal economic system was administered by noblemen who ruled over the serfs and justified their oppressive reign by arguing that God wanted them to rule, which is why they had been born into positions of power. The majority of serfs were illiterate; their education was restricted to church catechisms, and that was only if they were lucky enough to have received any education at all. Their horizons usually stretched only to the nearest market town. Their freedom of movement was so restricted that even if serfs had a desire to travel, they could not legally do so.

Stonemasons were in some ways a privileged and unique caste in the medieval world. Unlike most serfs, stonemasons were free men, bound to no lord and free to travel anywhere they chose. Stonemasons were educated, particularly in the mathematical and architectural theories pioneered by the Greeks and Romans. Using these skills, stonemasons constructed some of the most intricate, ornate, and sizeable buildings the world had ever seen, Gothic cathedrals. These structures were so large and complex that literally decades were spent constructing them. The Lincoln Cathedral, for example, was completed in 1311 after 126 years of construction, and was the tallest building in the world for 238 years. Compared to the average peasant, the knowledge of the stonemasons was powerful. As one can imagine, becoming a stonemason would have seemed an attractive path for intelligent and curious non-noblemen who were not content to remain resigned to a life of serfdom.

Young boys who wanted to become stonemasons had to first apprentice themselves to a Master Mason. There were no classes to take or manuals to read. Knowledge was acquired by painstaking experience. Apprentices were at the mercy of both their masters and other master stonemasons. They followed their masters from job-site to job-site, sometimes going for long stretches of time without work. If they were lucky, their masters would be hired on a cathedral project that would keep them employed for possibly their entire lives. When a stonemason was accepted into a particular worksite, he fell into an organizational structure that was remarkably similar to our Speculative Lodges.

The bands of Masons employed at a work-site were free men in the employ of the church, lord, or king who happened to be funding the project. The clergy and the nobility had very little control over the Masons; Masons were independent and organized themselves into an archaic union. The head of this union was the Master Mason. He was in charge of designing the cathedral, organizing the work of the Masons in his troop, negotiating with the funder of the project, and keeping harmony among the Masons on his worksite. Keeping harmony among the brethren was particularly difficult when the Masons met en masse at their worksite Lodge. Lodges of that period were multipurpose buildings. It was here that the Master Mason sketched his designs, Masons crafted stone to be used in the project, and more importantly, where Masons met as a group to debate the project and their pay, and inspected apprentices to see if they were worthy of promotion.

The apprentice process was complex. Once promoted, apprentices could expect standard stonemason wages, and if they chose they could then take apprentices of their own. As they traveled to different worksites, they would be vouched for by other Masons, and if necessary, could prove their skills by making a master's piece for the gathered brethren. The process of turning an apprentice into a stonemason took years, spanning the time a boy turned into a man. Becoming a stonemason was no guarantee of becoming a Master Mason; this honor was only reserved for the most talented stonemason. The Lodges of the day were temporary structures. Once a project was finished the stonemasons frequently moved on in search of more work, and Lodges generally disbanded.

There are numerous theories about how this system of operative stonemasons and Lodges would eventually evolve into modern Speculative Freemasonry. Lack of documentation and hard facts make the discovery of the origin of Speculative Masonry elusive. Though Anderson attempted to create a link to ancient times, scant evidence using modern historical, archeological, sociological, or anthropological methods has been found that would link the modern institution of Freemasonry to ancient Egypt, Greece or any other ancient civilization. Speculative Masonry began at some point in the late Middle Ages or early Renaissance era. The when is not so much in question. It is the who, how, and why that befuddle historians. While wild speculation exists on our origins, from ancient Egyptian rites to the Knights Templar, the best theory supported by the most legitimate historical evidence is rather more mundane.

Throughout the sixteenth century, the stonemason trade began to decline precipitously. The rise of both Protestantism and Puritanism in England transformed images of cathedrals from beautiful monuments to the glory of God, to dangerous symbols of popery and vanity. Construction of them ceased, and puritan zealots vandalized many. This lack of work drove many stonemasons into other professions and out of Lodges. To compensate for this, men who were not stonemasons were invited to join Lodges for the first time. These first Speculative Masons were almost always men of quality or nobility. Murray Lyon, an expert on Scottish Freemasonry put it thusly:

> *"Their admission to fellowship in an institution composed of operative Masons associated together for purposes of their craft, would, in all probability, originate in a desire to elevate its positions and increase its influence, and once adopted the system would further recommend itself to the fraternity by the opportunities which it presented for cultivating the friendship and enjoying the society of gentleman to whom, in an ordinary circumstances, there was little chance of their ever being personally known."* [17]

This process, whereby Operative Masonry turned into Speculative, first began in Scotland. Scottish Freemasonry is the oldest that can be historically identified. Several Lodges there are in possession of minutes that date back to the year 1600 AD. The oldest authenticated document relating to the raising of a non-operative Mason is dated June 8, 1600, when John Boswell, the Laird of Auchinleck, became a Mason. Historians are fairly certain that non-operative Masons were allowed into Lodges earlier than 1600. But modern historical practices can only say for certain what is documented, and even then this can be rife with speculation and innuendo.

As more and more speculative brethren entered Lodges, they ceased to be impromptu worksite meeting halls but instead geographically tied institutions. Eventually the Speculative Brothers began to outnumber the Operative and thus a new institution of gentlemen, merchants and laborers who metaphorically worked in the quarry of the mind was born. While initially confined to Scotland, Speculative Masonry began to seep south into England. York possessed a Speculative Lodge in 1693, and London Lodges are documented shortly thereafter.

On June 24, 1717, four London Lodges gathered at the Goose and Gridiron alehouse in St. Paul's churchyard to form a compact of mutual association. This association, called Grand Lodge, was to have jurisdiction over all four London Masonic Lodges and create a set of standard regulations for all four Lodges. This milestone is usually cited as the birth of Freemasonry, as from this point forward we can document the growth of the Fraternity with absolute certainty. As grand as its ambitions and titles were, Grand Lodge, in its early years, was marked by strife, secession, and general dysfunction. Early leaders such as George Payne, John Theophilus Desaguliers, and James Anderson synthesized the older traditions of the English stonemason Lodges and the early Scottish Speculative Lodges with new enlightenment ideals to create a new Masonic philosophy and code of conduct that is unique and remains unbroken for three centuries.

The Charges of a Freemason, which can be found within the *Constitutions of the Freemasons*, are the clearest example of this new philosophy. The Charges to every Freemason were, in part,

> *"Concerning god and religion a Mason is obligated by his tenure, to obey the moral law, and if he rightly understands the art, he will never be a stupid atheist nor a irreligious libertine, … tis now thought more expedient only to oblige them to that religion in which all men agree, leaving their particular opinions to themselves; this, to be good men and true or men of honor and honesty by whatever denominations or persuasions they may be distinguished. The persons admitted members of a lodge must be good and true men, free born and of mature and discreet age, no bondmen, no women, no immoral or scandals men but of good report. All Masons are as brethren upon the same level, yet Masonry takes no honor from a man that had before, nay rather it adds to his honor."* [18]

So from its inception Masonry accepted all men who express a belief in deity. Whomever or whatever they choose to worship is of no consequence to a Mason. Masons would also be men of upright moral character who show respect for one another regardless of rank and privilege, and believe that adherence to these principles brings honor to one's character. But perhaps most interesting of all is how these Masonic charges dealt with men who had committed rebellious actions against governments. Anderson writes,

"Of the civil magistrates a Mason is a peaceable subject to the civil powers, wherever and is never to be concerned in plots and conspiracies against the peace and welfare of the nation, ... if a brother should be a rebel against the state he is not to be countenanced in his rebellion, however he may be pitied as an unhappy man, and if convicted of no other crime, cannot be expelled from the lodge and his relation to it remains defensible." [19]

This clause in the constitution was probably added out of political necessity rather than philosophical belief. London, in 1717, was only thirty years removed from a political and religious revolution. In 1688, an unpopular Catholic monarch had been overthrown and replaced by a Protestant claimant to the throne of England. In 1717, the year Grand Lodge was formed, London was a tense mix of Catholic, Protestant, and Jewish residents who held little regard for one another. Many of the older Brothers in the Lodges of London had probably taken part in the revolution that had put a Protestant king on the throne. To ban men who had revolted against the government would have removed from Lodges some of their more senior members. It also would have removed the ability for politically minded Masons to engage in revolutionary activities like their forefathers had done. Interestingly, in this tense situation, Anderson found it important enough to reassure Brothers that this ancient prerogative would not be taken away by joining Freemasonry.

During this period of time, Lodges were being formed all over the world. A Masonic Lodge was founded in Boston in 1720, India in 1730, South Africa in 1770, Sydney in 1803, and Colombia in 1808. Thus, less than one hundred years after its official beginnings, Freemasonry had come to reside on every inhabited continent of the world. Wherever Masons met, they brought their radical ideas of religious tolerance and individual equality and freedom. Freemasonry conformed to the local practices and unique ideologies wherever it planted roots, but these basic tenets were never changed. North American Freemasonry arguably became the most successful branch of the Craft, and followed a unique path of its own.

Pre-revolutionary Freemasonry in North America was at first reserved for colonial elites. Soon, however, Lodges were opened to the burgeoning American middle class; men without birth or station who managed to achieve success through hard work and merit. Within Lodges, aristocrats and this new American middle class mixed together socially for the first time.

Even throughout the period of the American Revolution, Masonry continued to grow and prosper. Massachusetts established nineteen new Lodges during the revolution. St. Andrews Lodge, in the heart of Boston, raised almost one hundred new Brothers between 1777 and 1780. Freemasons were closely linked to the revolution and many served bravely in its armed forces. The archives of St. Georges Lodge in Schenectady, New York, reveal that seventy-seven of its 134 members served in the continental army.[20]

Freemasonry played an important role in the continental army. Standard convention of the time suggested that one's military rank would reflect one's social prominence. As John Adams wrote to Nathanial Greene, the general in charge of the operations of the continental army in the southern states,

> *"A general officer, ought to be a gentleman of letters and general knowledge, a man of address and knowledge of the world he should carry with him authority and command."*[21]

While this sentiment rigidly governed military affairs in Europe, the American revolutionary army officer corps was largely made of men who would not be considered elite in civilian life. These new officers were often anxious about this lack of status. The Ritual and teachings of Freemasonry offered training in manners, honor, and knowledge in the seven liberal arts and sciences that all gentlemen were expected to master. In this way, Freemasonry gave these new officers the support and recommendation they needed to live up to the expectations society placed on them.

The universalism Masonry espoused had other tangible benefits for continental army officers. Officers could expect that the Fraternity would protect them if the opposing side captured them. If they were killed on the battlefield, the two sides would often come together to host joint Masonic funerals. As one famous Freemason wrote to another Brother who happened to be an enemy officer,

> *"As masons we are disarmed of that resentment which stipulates to undistinguished desolation; and however our political sentiments may impel us in the public dispute, we are still brethren, and (our professional duty apart) out to promote the happiness of each other."* [22]

After the war, when many Masonic ideals were folded into the new philosophy of the American government, membership in Freemasonry soared. As Steven Bullock, author of *Revolutionary Brotherhood: Freemasonry and the Transformation of the American Social Order*, describes,

> *"The new vision of the fraternity fitted into the widely shared desire to reconceive the character of the American society as it emerged from the Revolution. By celebrating morality and individual merit, Masonry seemed to exemplify the ideals necessary to build a society based on virtue*

and liberty. Fraternal membership and ideology helped bring high standing to a broad range of Americans, breaking down the artificial boundaries of birth and wealth. Masonry offered participation in both the great classical tradition of civilization and the task of building a new nation..... Lodges offered moral instruction without sectarian divisions, a symbolic language of social distinction that did not depend upon local associations. Through membership in a fraternity that ignored or rejected traditional boundaries and divisions, officers built a larger republican identity that rejected the colonist's localism.... Masons thus did more than lay the republics physical cornerstones, they also helped form the symbolic foundations of what the Great Seal called, "the new order for the ages." [23]

The Fraternity's most important role in this new republican nation was to teach morality to its citizens. Since The Enlightenment, political theorists have written about what qualities a leader of men should possess. This type of virtuous and moral education was considered essential for the various princes, kings, queens, earls, emirs, czars, and caliphs who ruled over Europe because of the amount of influence they wielded over the citizens under their rule. In this new republican government, however, the people themselves were their own rulers. Therefore it was imperative that the citizenry themselves be trained in morality, so that the nation would not devolve into a form of unenlightened mob rule. While churches were traditionally viewed as the formal teachers of morality and virtue, their wide sectarian differences deemed them unfit to be the teachers to a nation with no official religion. At that time, schools were not universally available and much of the population was illiterate. Freemasonry, through its nonsectarian philosophy and use of oral rituals, transcended these limitations.

This was a Golden Age for Freemasonry. Lodges had purpose and a mission. Just as operative stonemasons built cathedrals, speculative Freemasons inculcated societies with soaring ideals and new ideas. In mythology, when Icarus in his hubris flew too close to the sun, his hand-fashioned wings melted and Icarus fell to earth to his death. In some ways Freemasonry has suffered the same fate. Since Freemasonry was seen as part of the enlightened new order, many of its members became the leaders of the new American government. Freemasons' bold humanitarian assertions and immense political power at all levels of government made the Fraternity unpopular in some circles. This anti-Masonic sentiment would become empowered and unleashed by a crime in a rural upstate New York town which ultimately became known as the Morgan Affair.

William Morgan was a wandering stonemason from Culpepper, Virginia, who settled both himself and his family in the small town of Batavia, New York, located thirty miles west of Rochester. It is unclear in what way Morgan was affiliated with his local Lodge. Some say he was a Master Mason while others believe he was merely an imposter. Regardless, Morgan made it clear that he was intent on publishing a book detailing all of Masonry's secret rituals, words, and symbols. Before this could occur, Morgan was abducted by a group of men and was never seen again. It has been speculated that he was murdered by Freemasons to protect their secret society. This ignited virulent anti-Masonic sentiment that was unleashed upon the entire country. This movement, which spawned the United States first powerful third political party, was a critique of the perceived power Freemasonry wielded in this country.

When the dust settled, in 1838, Freemasonry was practically destroyed in several states and severely weakened everywhere. In fact, the Fraternity ceased to exist entirely in Vermont and Michigan. New York Freemasonry saw over three quarters of its 228 Lodges dissolve. Kentucky Freemasonry saw the number of Lodges drop from fifty to eleven between 1826 and 1836.[24]

More significantly for us today, the anti-Masonic movement in the early part of the nineteenth century humbled and significantly changed American Freemasonry. Early American Freemasonry had viewed itself and its members as a key foundation piece of the new American republic. Freemasonry, after the Morgan Affair, was a more domesticated organization. Its membership eventually recovered, but the Fraternity was no longer a revolutionary movement. Instead it became more of a Victorian gentleman's club focused on the more symbolic aspects of the Ritual and the charitable and fraternal aspects of the Craft. As Albert Pike, one of the most cited Masonic authors of all time, noted a half century after the Morgan Affair, Freemasonry had "gained popularity, while losing its right to reverence." [25]

Freemasonry would have to wait another 120 years before the Fraternity regained the prominence it had enjoyed before the Morgan Affair.

The late 1940s to early 1960s marked a high point in American civic and religious engagement that resulted in a golden age for American fraternal societies such as Freemasonry, the Loyal Order of Moose, Kiwanis, The Knights of Columbus, and the United Order of Odd Fellows. In 1959 there were four million Masons in the United States.[26] While all age groups experienced this high period of civic engagement, those in their twenties were particularly engaged with their community institutions at that time. For example, between 1950 and 1957, the number of young adults attending church in America increased by over twenty percentage points. Membership in Freemasonry rose 10 percent in that same time period.[27] At its height in 1959, 12 percent of all American males belonged to the Fraternity. These Brothers were the architects of the magnificent Lodges and fraternal infrastructure we enjoy today.

The majority of those Brothers were World War II veterans, men who had bled and sacrificed in the snow of the Ardennes and in the steaming jungles of the South Pacific. When they came home to America after the war, these same men built one of the most prosperous societies in the history of the world. The defining characteristics of this generation were patriotism, personal discipline, loyalty, humility, and, most of all, an emphasis on cultural conformity. These men flocked to Lodges to experience the sense of fraternalism and purpose they had experienced in their units during the war. The intellectual pursuits that had defined parts of the Fraternity since its inception, were no longer priorities. As one Brother wrote in a 1959 article in Philalethes magazine,

> *"A word on the ritual. Time was when the drama of our ritual was the only entertainment in the community and the only opportunity for self-expression of our members. T.V., movies and sport spectacles now furnish the former, and service clubs, toastmaster clubs and theater guilds satisfy the inner yearning to be an actor. Let us consider the ritual and its place in our Order. That there has been an overemphasis on the ritual and ritualists; I believe most Masonic leaders will agree. Men will no longer come back to meeting after meeting simply to re-hear the ritual"* [28]

By the 1960s the candidates joining Lodges reflected the changing American culture. The values of the greatest generation, particularly the emphasis on cultural conformity, were rejected as archaic and intolerant. This new generation possessed a radically different worldview than their parents, but they were still drawn to fraternal orders like the Freemasons. Both the greatest generation and the early baby boomers believed in a "public spirited universalism." They believed that public policy and the greater culture should be working toward a common good.

World War II, the Civil Rights movement, the creation of the Peace Corps, and space exploration all reflect this universalism. World War II was an experience shared by almost the entire country. Men, women, and children of all races and religions sacrificed for the same common goal. When Neil Armstrong walked on the moon in July of 1969, it reflected mankind's innate desire to explore the world, or in this case the universe, around us. The Peace Corps captured the imagination of America's young people who wished to altruistically spread America's material prosperity to the rest of the world. And while the Civil Rights movement was certainly not universal in its popularity, its tenets reflected the values of universalism. Its advocates believed every human being deserved basic human rights and dignity.

Since the end of this golden age, our membership has declined by over 70 percent in the following decades. It is well known in Masonic circles that the last thirty years has been a disastrous time for Freemasonry in North America.

The later part of the 1960s and early part of the 1970s saw another dramatic shift in American culture. The public-spirited universalism that drove the greatest generation and the early part of the baby boomers vanished in the hellish din of the Vietnam War, the Watergate scandal, racial and student upheaval, and the assassinations of inspirational figures such as President John Kennedy and Reverend Martin Luther King Jr. The economic collapse of the 1970s further contributed to this societal upheaval.

Robert Putnam, one of America's most renowned sociologists described this culture shift thusly:

> *"America's Cultural Revolution proved less lethal than Mao's' but more enduring."* [29]

Public-spirited universalism would gradually be replaced by private self-fulfillment through more material means. This would have a dramatic effect on both the popularity of Freemasonry and the character of the men who would soon populate its Lodges. Sydney Ahlstrom, an American sociologist writing in the late 1960s, accurately summarized what was happening to American culture at the time:

> *"The decade of the Sixties was a time, in short, when the old foundations of national confidence, patriotic idealism, moral traditionalism and even historic Judeo-Christian theism were awash. Presuppositions that had held firm for century's even millennia were being widely questioned. The existence of a basic shift of mood rooted in deep social and institutional dislocations was anything but ephemeral….it was perfectly clear to any reasonable observant American that the postwar revival of the Eisenhower years had completely sputtered out, and that the nation was experiencing a crisis of conscience of unprecedented depth."* [30]

This transformation was complete by the mid-1990s. The rise of the Internet has accelerated this transition, with almost every product, service, and social interaction available from the comfort of your own home, and all available without any collaborative interaction with another human being.

In this new cultural environment, organizations such as the Freemasons held little value to the new generation of Americans. The greatest generation and early cohort of baby boomers continued to be active Freemasons, but as these men aged and started to pass away in record numbers, no younger Brothers were joining the Lodges to replace them.

The decades spanning the 1970s to the early 2000s are the lost years of modern Freemasonry. Membership plummeted, and in response our Fraternity changed in painful and ultimately futile ways to attract members, or worse yet, remained stagnant and stuck fifty years in the past. Lodges exacerbated the situation by doubling down on the activities that attracted early boomers to Lodge, such as fellowship and charity, while destroying large segments of the Masonic tradition that appealed to younger candidates. Initiatives were enacted so that candidates would no longer have to pass proficiency, cheapening the Degree process and the Ritual to the point of almost making it irrelevant. In a similar manner, the intellectual, spiritual, and revolutionary aspects were shorn from Freemasonry. Lodges began to fail as the Fraternity entered a dark age that rivaled the Morgan Affair era. It is only now that we are just beginning to crawl out of this darkness and back toward the light.

THE
OBSERVANCE
MOVEMENT

IN 1982 A WANDERING NEW ZEALANDER WITH a penchant for amateur mysticism, historical research, and religious study published a work of amateur history that would have an explosive, albeit unintended, effect on the revival of Freemasonry in North America.

Michael Baigent was by all accounts a charming man who had ventured over half the world in pursuit of the sacred and mysterious. He spent much of his life studying and comparing the world's great religions. In the course of his travels and studying, he believed he had uncovered a great conspiracy that had been hidden from the world for two millennia.

Baigent, along with coauthors Richard Leigh and Henry Lincoln, published *Holy Blood and Holy Grail: Shocking Secrets and the Legacy of the Grail* with the goal of shocking the foundations of western religion to its core. The book argues that the historical Jesus Christ married sometime between the ages of sixteen and thirty-three. After the persecution of Jesus and his followers at the hands of the Romans, his wife and children fled ancient Israel. They eventually settled in a small Jewish community in Southern France. For over four hundred years this bloodline was preserved in France. Thereafter, this holy bloodline intermarried with the royal family of the Franks, then known as the Merovingians. Then, shortly before the turn of the fifth century, the Catholic Church pledged itself in perpetuity to this royal bloodline, knowing full well the divine that dwelled within the Merovingians' bloodline. However, in a series of assassinations and political machinations, the Church ultimately betrayed the Merovingians, and bloodily sought to eradicate the bloodline and suppress any who had knowledge of it.

Against all odds, the bloodline survived, protected by a secret society called the Priory of Sion. The goal of the Priory was to become divine rulers through intermarriage and political intrigue. They sought to erode the spiritual hegemony of the Church by fostering esoteric societies like the Rosicrucians, and of course, Freemasonry. The book further speculates that the secret Priory of Sion and a modern, though unknown Merovingian are conspiring in the present day to establish a theocratic Pan-European confederation ruled by a dynasty descended from Jesus. They state that the Priory is a well-connected and extremely well-funded organization, which, since 1956, has sought to increase its membership fourfold in what can only be a buildup for a new initiative aimed at securing substantial political power.

Although widely criticized by respected theologians and historians, *Holy Blood, Holy Grail* very quickly became a worldwide bestseller. Over four million copies were sold and distributed, and the BBC produced a widely viewed television documentary.

Though the theory never gained wide acceptance, *Holy Blood, Holy Grail* began to change the paradigm in which the greater public began to view Freemasonry. In *Holy Blood, Holy Grail*, certain Masonic rites were declared to have a direct link to the ancient Near Eastern religion of Manichaeism as well as the fourteenth century organization of warrior monks known as the Knights Templar.

The work also claimed that Freemasonry is composed of two different castes: A lower class of regular initiates interested in esoteric thought and charitable good works, and a higher order of men who were initiated into a secret Degree whereby they swore allegiance to a group of superiors. This is the elite group, the book claims, that belonged to the Priory of Sion.

The authors speculate that this is why Pope Clement XII issued his famous papal bull in 1738, banning Catholics from joining Freemasonry. Whether for good or evil, the authors believed Freemasonry possessed certain secrets of the ancient world. On the heels of *Holy Blood, Holy Grail* came a series of extremely popular books and movies that cast Freemasons and Freemasonry in general in a similar light.

The most popular and well known of this group is the Robert Langdon series written by Dan Brown, including *The Da Vinci Code*, *Angels and Demons*, and *The Lost Symbol*. The *National Treasure* film series is another example in this style.

Freemasons began to be portrayed as an enlightened secret society, shielding ancient secrets and wisdom from evil men who would use them for power or financial profit. Perhaps the work most associated with this style is Dan Brown's third Robert Langdon novel, *The Lost Symbol*. To save a friend, Robert Langdon must locate "the lost word of Master Mason." In Masonic legend, "the word" was lost when Hiram Abiff, the great architect of Solomon's Temple, was murdered outside the East Gate of Jerusalem over two millennia ago. Langdon is forced into this quest by a Master Mason who joined the Craft believing the Master's word would grant him unlimited power. In an open letter to global Freemasonry, Brown expressed his appreciation for the group thusly:

> *"In a world where men do battle over whose definition of god is most accurate, I cannot adequately express the deep respect and admiration I feel toward an organization in which men of differing faiths are able to break bread together in a bond of Brotherhood, friendship and camaraderie"* [31]

This admiration for Freemasonry comes across in Mr. Brown's robust research of the Craft and the poetic language with which he describes its role. In fact, Mr. Brown has probably written the best description of the philosophy behind Freemasonry by a non-Mason. This wonderful depiction of Masonic philosophy can be found in *The Lost Symbol*. Peter Solomon, a Master Mason and Robert Langdon's mentor, explains his devotion to the Craft in the following way:

> *"We've lost the word, and yet its true meaning is still within reach, right before our eyes. It exists in all the enduring texts from the Bible to Bhagavad-Gita to the Koran and beyond. All of these texts are revered upon the altars of Freemasonry because Masons understand what the world seems to have forgotten, that each of these texts in its own way is quietly whispering the exact same message, know ye not that ye are gods."* [32]

The result of this intense exposure in the popular media made Freemasonry, for a brief time, popular. Young men flocked to Lodges in search of the esoteric secrets Freemasonry supposedly had possessed since ancient times. While anecdotal, I believe the example of my local Lodge can once again be instructive. The year before the release of *The Da Vinci Code* and *National Treasure,* my Lodge raised six new Brothers. The year in which those two popular culture phenomena were released, my Lodge raised *sixteen* new Brothers. [33]

This was certainly a positive development for Lodges; an infusion of young and enthusiastic blood was unquestionably needed. But there is an old saying: once out of the frying pan, you don't want to find yourself in the fire. While Lodges began feeling optimistic about turning the tide regarding declining membership, some astute Brothers began to notice a disturbing trend.

These new Brothers entering Lodges were initially quite enthusiastic about joining the Fraternity. In many cases, however, their enthusiasm quickly tapered off, and often within three to five years after initiation, they stopped coming to Lodge entirely. Thereafter, many quietly left Freemasonry forever.

What was driving this phenomenon? As with any complex question, there is often no simple answer. However, some Masonic thinkers have put forth a theory. The popular culture provided a teasing buildup of anticipation. These men were entering the Fraternity expecting something secret, divine, mysterious, and out of the ordinary. With such a buildup, it is easy to be disappointed. Often times they found something mundane at best, and at worst something dull and repetitive. The Craft simply was not ready for these new Brothers, who were motivated by something quite different than Brothers of the previous generation.

In response to this cognitive dissonance, a group of Brothers proposed a cause and a solution. They proposed that this gap in expectations was caused by the stagnation of modern Freemasonry, and what was needed was a restoration of the Craft's former glory. They believed in returning Freemasonry to its roots in the seventeenth and eighteenth century. They stated that Freemasonry once again should highlight its philosophical and ritualistic aspects while downplaying the fraternal and charitable motifs of the Craft.

This group coalesced in North America in 2001, and founded the Masonic Restoration Foundation. Together they published a series of articles and books that outlined a strategic plan for individual Lodges so that they could begin the process of restoring the Craft to reverence and therefore a state of relevance. Eventually these Lodges became known as Traditional Observance, or Observant Lodges.

Today there are close to fifty Observant Lodges, and they can be found in twenty-five states and four Canadian provinces. Observant Lodges try to create an environment that is conducive to deep philosophical inquiries and spiritual growth. The Victorian gentleman's ideal of good times and charity is mostly absent from Observant Lodge's Trestleboards. Instead these lodges have chosen to focus on the esoteric and philosophic features of the Craft.

Perhaps the best document that specifies what separates an Observant Lodge from other Lodges is entitled *The Eight Steps to Excellence: The Observant Lodge*, written by W.B Andrew Hammer of Alexandria, Virginia. This paper includes many of the same ideas as Mr. Hammer's book, *Observing the Craft: The Pursuit of Excellence in Masonic Labor and Observance*. Brother Hammer very articulately lays out eight specific points that differentiate Observant Lodges from other Lodges. His points range from membership and progressive lines to proficiency in Masonic Ritual and beyond. The paraphrased and much truncated eight points are as follows:

• **Guarding the West Gate:** Masonry was never meant to be a mass-market product. Masonry is not for every man. Only a small number of men are truly committed to beginning the journey that Freemasonry truly requires. Therefore, some Observant Lodges have membership caps to ensure that their Lodges do not expand artificially and remain small groups of like-minded men. When an individual petitions the Lodge for membership, a very thorough investigation is made of his readiness to become a Mason. Just as a Master inspects a potential apprentice, so should the brethren inspect this man stringently and objectively. If he does not meet the high standards of the Lodge, he is not allowed to enter. This changes the culture of desperation that has pervaded the Fraternity for the past forty years. By being exclusive, an Observant Lodge assures its candidates are both highly motivated and interested.

• **Being Proficient in Masonic Ritual and Law:** The Ritual of Freemasonry is the central axis upon which the Fraternity is supported. Without the Ritual we would not have our guiding morals and values. Masonic Ritual and law are what separate modern Freemasonry from other organizations like the Rotarians or Kiwanis. All Masons, but especially officers and those who help perform Degree work, should be actively engaging the Ritual so as to better understand its teachings. Proficiency needs to be attained to enact Ritual in a way that is both awe inspiring and accurate for the brethren. This requires both time and energy, and should be viewed as part of the Masonic journey.

• **A Commitment to Advancing Brethren through the Degrees by Mutual and Genuine Effort:** I have already discussed how Freemasonry lost many of its members in the decades spanning 1970 to 2000. In response to this crisis, North American Freemasonry began to implement a set of reforms that they believed would bolster failing membership numbers. These reforms made it much easier to become a Mason. (A good example of this was the "One Day Class System" where it became possible to go "all the way in one day.") Traditionally a candidate was exposed to the Degrees in a multi month journey that could only be completed by passing proficiency in the Masonic catechism. In a One Day Class, a man could come to a weekend session in the morning and walk out that same night having seen all three Degrees, and be in possession of all of Freemasonry's most important secret grips and words. All of this would be bestowed upon a candidate without him having to demonstrate any proficiency in Masonic Ritual or commitment to its values. Observant Lodges believe that achieving light in Masonry should require effort, just like attaining any other valuable commodity. Observant Lodges not only require candidates to be proficient in the Masonic catechism, but also require candidates to present a paper in open Lodge detailing the philosophical lessons or observations that were most meaningful to them. This process often takes a year or more for completion.

• **The Selection and Advance of Officers Should Be by Merit Alone:** Most Masonic Lodges elect officers using the progressive line system. The officer line is made up of all the elected Masonic officer positions. When in line, unless he has committed an egregious offense, a Brother can expect to be "promoted" each year through unopposed elections until eventually he is Master. To get in line, a Brother is usually screened by a group of respected older Brothers who decide on the candidate's qualifications to eventually govern the Lodge. The majority of the Lodge really has no say in the process. This has led to sometimes accurate accusations of the Craft being an "old boys club," where progressive ideas and younger members can be stifled. Observant Lodges believe that while done for expediency and efficiency sake, a progressive line circumvents Masonry's democratic roots. In some Observant Lodges, each elected position is voted upon in a general election. While this may be cumbersome it ensures a healthy competition for central roles, and may prevent incompetent leadership.

• **Dressing Your Best for Lodge:** Some jurisdictions recently have argued that Masonic Lodges should not require a dress code. Philosophically it is argued that aprons in the seventeenth and eighteenth centuries were "blue collar," and often-times dirty work attire; our ancient brethren would not have been opposed to such attire being worn in modern Lodges. Observant Lodges believe that your state of dress indicates the level of respect and reverence you have for an occasion or event. A Lodge meeting should be special, and therefore you should dress accordingly. Observant Lodges insist that members and visitors wear a tuxedo and white gloves to Lodge meetings. Dressing formally accomplishes two important things. It helps establish that sense of awe that Masonic meetings should instill, and it helps instill the proper respect a Mason should have for his work.

• **A Lodge Must Offer Quality Assemblies and Be Willing to Pay for Them:** In keeping with the theme that a Masonic meeting is a special event, Lodges must offer their members a reason to come to a Lodge meeting by providing memorable programs. In practice this means a raise in dues and a raise in the amount the Lodge spends on meals and guest speakers. The justification is that quality programs offer Brothers a valuable experience and a reason to look forward to coming to Lodge. Freemasonry competes in the marketplace of how members spend their time and energy. When that concept is recognized, upgrading Lodge programs to attract Brothers from friends, families and other activities makes sense.

• **The Return of a Sense of Awe to Our Ceremonies:** Masonic ceremonies should be used to create a uniquely contemplative atmosphere for Brothers. Ritual, when done well, creates a feeling of awe and wonder. It is for this reason that ritual is employed in religious ceremonies, sporting events, and almost every other form of organized group activity. Ritual provides structure, order, and purpose. Masonry's Ritual has this capacity. Observant Lodges use music, the manipulation of light and darkness, incense, and other strategies with the goal of creating a sensory and emotional experience.

• **Masonic Education at Every Meeting:** It is not good enough to offer quality and entertaining programming if the programs themselves are not educational in nature. Freemasonry is based on the idea of quarrying in the mind and in doing so finding spiritual and intellectual fulfillment or "light." If Freemasonry is not providing a venue for education, philosophical or otherwise, it is failing in one of its oldest and primary purposes.

The creation of Observant Lodges has created quite a stir in modern Freemasonry. Proponents and detractors have at times forgotten their obligation of Brotherly love, and descended into vitriolic diatribes against one another. Some zealous advocates of Observant Lodges have come to believe that anything less than their style is simply not Masonry while defensive detractors level the charge of elitism and sowing division in the Craft against the Observance Movement.

At the end of the day, however, how a Masonic Lodge investigates its candidates, what its membership goals are, how proficient the members are in Masonic law and Ritual, how and when a Lodge passes a candidate from one Degree to the next, how a Lodge elects its officers, how its members dress and what it requires from its members in dues payments, are ultimately determined by the individuals who work in those Lodges.

The infinite combinations of how a Lodge conducts itself are part of what makes the Fraternity so interesting and why traveling from jurisdiction to jurisdiction can be so rewarding. And let me be clear, all of these practices can be described as legitimate flavors of Freemasonry. Whether a Lodge lights its Lodge room with candlelight or fluorescents is ultimately a minor difference that is determined by the individual Lodges. While these differences are important, the infinite number of variations makes generalizations on "best practice" ultimately futile, for what may meet the needs of one Lodge may be detrimental to another.

The true divide is not between Observant Lodges and everybody else. The real divide in twenty-first century Freemasonry is between those who want Freemasonry to become even more a service organization centered on social interaction and fork and knife Degrees, and those who believe that Freemasonry should return to an emphasis on spirituality, esoteric learning, an ancient initiatic tradition, and a belief that Freemasonry should play a role in inspiring its members to fight for it Masonic values outside of the Lodge room.

Both traditions can be found in Masonry's past, but the two traditions are in many ways antithetical to each other. More and more Lodges are choosing to focus on one tradition or the other. Lodges that are dividing their energies between the two are most likely doing neither well. This divide is increasingly taking on a generational component. Once again, my Lodge can provide anecdotal evidence to illustrate this fact.

Brother Solomon is a young man just beginning to travel down the path of adulthood. In his late twenties, Brother Solomon has no family of his own though he does plan to marry his current girlfriend in the near future. Brother Solomon is a man of modest means, a very middle-class individual. Brother Solomon was raised Catholic, but both he and his family never put much emphasis on faith during his childhood, and while he celebrates Christian holidays, his spirituality is ill defined.

Brother Solomon joined Freemasonry because he believed that the Craft could offer him a venue in which he could learn about himself. He believed that the rituals and teachings of Freemasonry would offer him a level of sacredness he had yet to experience outside of the Craft. Brother Solomon jumped into the ritualistic aspects of our Lodge soon after his raising. He began volunteering for various roles in the Degrees almost immediately. He began to read books about the ancient traditions of Freemasonry. After a visit to an Observant Lodge, Brother Solomon remarked that, "I feel like I have just driven a Ferrari after driving a Chevy most of my life." He is currently involved in creating a local Observant Lodge in his district. He is not disinterested in the charitable actions our Lodge takes on; he just feels that is not what he joined Freemasonry to do.

In contrast to Brother Solomon is Brother John. Brother John is in his late fifties, and has been in the Craft for over thirty years. Brother John is a retiree with a longtime wife, two kids, and even a few grandchildren. Brother John is an incredibly generous man. He will give you the shirt off his back if you asked for it. Brother John is the type of man who will show up at every event organized by the Lodge, large or small. He will flip pancakes or burgers, cut firewood, help you move, and clean dishes. The only thing Brother John will not do is learn any portion of the Ritual he is not required to. Again, it is not that he is disinterested in the Masonic Ritual; it is just not why he joined the Craft. Brother John joined Freemasonry for fellowship and the possibility of helping those in his community. His spirituality is defined by his lifelong membership in a Christian church where he is in attendance every week.

More and more these two Brothers will eventually begin to gravitate to Lodges that fit their diametric desires for the Craft.

Brother Solomon would leap at the opportunity to join a solemn, academic, and ritual-oriented Observance Lodge. Brother John would abhor the very same thing that would attract Brother Solomon. Again, both Brothers are practicing Freemasonry, just in different ways.

I have already stated that I believe millennials are not interested in joining the Victorian service club that Freemasonry transformed into after the Morgan Affair.

I believe most millennials who are drawn to Freemasonry will continue to be attracted to Observant or ritual-oriented Lodges. Social or service Lodges will continue to survive, and a few will even thrive. But eventually those Lodges will grow older, while Observant and other similar Lodges will continue to grow younger.

If we are interested in attracting the millennial generation into the Craft, ritual and esoteric thought will once again have to become a major point of emphasis for Lodges. Have Observant Lodges attained their goal of restoring Freemasonry to the historical and philosophical intent of its founders? In my opinion they have been successful only in part. While Freemasonry has always been diverse for some in the Fraternity, Freemasonry served two very unique and important roles in society.

The first was to codify an organization that through ancient symbols and mysteries educated men on the universalism and equality of all men in the eyes of the great architect of the universe.

The second was to see that members of that organization champion the enlightenment values on which Freemasonry was founded, so they would eventually supersede the antique and cruel medieval values that defined society at that time.

Once again it is interesting to note that almost all the democratic revolutions of the eighteenth and nineteenth centuries were led by Freemasons on several continents. While conspiracy theorists view this fact as proof of a worldwide plot by the Craft, the truth is far simpler. Those who inculcate the tenets of Freemasonry will be inspired to correct the ills of the world. The democratic revolutions of the eighteenth and nineteenth centuries are a direct outgrowth of this. Observant Lodges excel in creating a place where men can be educated using ancient symbols and mysteries, but like most current North American Lodges, utterly fail in the second role that used to define Freemasonry for many of our past brethren. I hope that there is a coming realization of that fact.

In February 2015 an article was published in the online magazine Laudable Pursuit entitled "Intentional Freemasonry." The article was written by Brother James Marshall, currently the secretary of Veritas Lodge, an Observant Lodge in Oklahoma. The article laments the current state of Lodges and Brothers who have little to do other than argue over bills or simply go through the motions of making new Brothers through the Degree process. As part of an exercise to correct this line of thinking, Brother Marshall and the Brothers of Veritas Lodge constructed a mission statement for themselves. In Brother Marshall's own words, the mission statement "has defined the purpose of my Lodge and has given its members, new and old, an ideal to intentionally strive for." The mission statement itself is as follows:

"We, the men of Veritas Lodge, in our endeavor to better ourselves in virtue, intellect, wisdom, and historical understanding, to explore a curiosity for mystery that all men hold, to promote the cause of liberty for all mankind, to guide other men into manhood through an initiatic

ritual and tradition, and to strengthen our fraternal bonds and our compassion for the world, have established our Lodge as a light added to light, thereby giving glory to our Creator." [34]

I believe this was a great example of a Lodge trying to encompass both the philosophical and social intent of early Freemasonry. I believe there are activities that Lodges can engage in that both honor the ancient Craft, and respect the sensibilities of Brothers who find the concept of engaging in those types of activities in Masonry antithetical to the organization's harmony.

This, I believe, is the missing key to unlocking a new renaissance of Masonic activity on this continent in the twenty-first century. My Lodge does its best to emphasize ritual, Masonic education, and esoteric thought. We try to incorporate many of the best practices of modern Freemasonry, and we routinely attract and initiate almost half a dozen young and enthusiastic men every year. And yet, the revolving door of young enthusiastic men entering the Lodge and leaving disillusioned continues. It is because we have only come half-way in restoring the Craft to its past reverence and relevance.

I have made some sweeping claims about what I believe millennials want out of Freemasonry. What is now needed is a portrait of the millennial generation. Only then can we look at how Freemasonry can fulfill certain desires unique to this generation.

The next chapter will examine millennials using a set of scientific studies conducted by professional pollsters and sociologists. If, as Masons, we fail to acknowledge the implications for our Craft that are revealed with this data, I foresee a bleak future of our beloved Fraternity further into the twenty-first century.

PORTRAIT OF A GENERATION

W HO ARE THESE MILLENNIALS WHO MIGHT be looking to join our Lodges? What makes them so unique? We need to compare and contrast them to the preceding generations. It is important to remember that the baby boomer generation changed everything. That is not a generalization or an exaggeration. Almost every facet of the American cultural landscape was changed forever when the boomers came of age and started to exercise their political and social capital.

Morals, values and other aspects of the American cultural landscape changed at a rapid and prolific pace, amounting to a profound social revolution. In addition to some bedrock American principles, other facets of American culture including music, economics, technology, government, environmental conservation, and increasingly, health care and the aging process all dramatically transformed thanks to the boomer influence.

Part of the reason that these changes became so pervasive was the sheer size of the baby boom. Over seventy-five million Americans are considered boomers. No proceeding generation had ever come close to approaching that figure, until now.

The millennial population currently stands at seventy-five million people and is expected to reach eighty-one million in 2036.[35] Both generations account for over a quarter of the nation. As millennials come of age, American society is poised to change once again at the behest of its largest cohort of citizens. Freemasonry has the potential to be on the cutting edge of this wave of change. Many facets of American culture are already beginning to mark this transition with new products, philosophies, and outreach measures.

Corporations are changing their benefits packages and their management style to keep pace with the rising numbers of millennials entering the workforce. It is estimated that by the year 2020, millennials will have become 50 percent of the worldwide labor force. Telecommuting, workplace inclusion, and flexible benefit packages including more vacation time in exchange for a lower wage are increasingly becoming the norm in corporate America. Nonprofits, charities, political parties, and businesses have changed their advertising strategies in order to reach more and more millennials. Since most millennials watch less traditional TV than the previous generation, increasingly outreach efforts have shifted to webisodes, blogs, and other interactive social media venues such as Twitter, Facebook, Vine, Instagram, and Tumblr.

One facet of American culture that has yet to feel the winds of millennial change is civic engagement. But that grace period may be coming to an end. A respected sociologist remarked on the coming societal shift in the following way:

> *"They know that all is not well in the world, the Boomer Generation knew that and protested it, Generation X knew that and was depressed about it, the Millennials know that but they believe they can have a role in changing it."* [36]

So how can we create a portrait of the millennial generation? It is impossible to create a single portrait of seventy-five million souls. Gross generalization is bound to be a problem. The following set of characteristics, of course, does not apply to every single millennial either currently sitting in or waiting to enter your Lodge. But there is quite a bit of documented evidence from very well respected sociologists and polling organizations that suggest the characteristics, opinions and beliefs listed below are shared by millions of millennials. It is also important to note that the list below contains only what is pertinent and useful for us in the Masonic Fraternity. Other touchstones of millennial culture such as workplace expectations, financial habits and musical tastes are not taken into account.

The hard data used in this chapter is gathered from several sources, some Masonic but mostly "civilian." Contributors include several Pew surveys, two bestselling-sociologists who have studied millennial culture and attitudes, several articles from the *Huffington Post*, *Forbes Magazine*, the Council of Economic Advisors to the President of the United States and a Masonic survey that encompassed millennial Masons in over thirty jurisdictions.

If we believe that attracting millennials is important to the future of the Craft, then it is important that we all understand what makes our target audience tick. An old business axiom states "If you're marketing to everybody, you are essentially marketing to nobody." A basic understanding of millennial traits and a willingness to enhance already existing Masonic principles and structures can lead to a boom of growth among this newest cohort of American men. The following list I believe is a great place to begin this journey of understanding.

Attitudes toward Parents, Authority Figures and Older Individuals: One of the most revolutionary characteristics of the millennial generation is that they generally tend to respect their parents, authority figures and many older adults. Millennials stand in stark contrast to their baby boomer parents, who confrontationally and boisterously protested against their professors, universities, government, police, church, and often times the attitudes of their own parents. While baby boomers collectively coined the phrase,

"Don't trust anybody over thirty," by contrast, millennials genuinely respect older adults:

• When asked which generation had more moral values, eight out of ten millennials chose an older generation.[36]

• 60 percent of all millennials actively seek out their parent's guidance when they have questions or concerns on various facets of adulthood.[37]

One of the more common, albeit misunderstood, critiques of modern Freemasonry is that sluggish old men heavily populate the Craft. Having so much gray hair in Lodge rooms is generally believed to be a turnoff for younger prospective Masons. In fact, it seems that millennials are uniquely inclined to respect and appreciate their elders. Helicopter parents and teachers raised millennials, thus an older mentor was always within reach if we had questions. Adults were never our adversaries, simply helpful, albeit sometimes overbearing, friends.

As one millennial Mason wrote,

"When I first started my journey, I clamored to my mentor and old college buddy for the first step. That's all I asked of him. After he suggested a couple of authors and a specific book, I was off to the races. Sometimes, we need to be instructed in how to take the first step."[38]

An older membership base does not tend to turn off younger members. If anything, they are turned off by the perception, and sometimes reality, that Masonry is a "good old boys club." When young men complain, they are not bemoaning age, but rather the feeling of exclusion from participation and leadership roles by older Brothers. As one frustrated Brother wrote.

"I'm sick of being looked at as naive because I am so young. I am sick of the "good old days" being behind us and I am tired of the older generation concluding that as a Millennial I have a sense of entitlement."
39

Diversity: Freemasonry was founded on the concept of religious tolerance and diversity. At the time of its founding, proponents of religious diversity were considered eccentric and metaphorically inhabited a small and isolated place in the political and social landscape.

While generally on the cutting edge of the social curve, Masons have never been immune to societal pressure and human failings. Particularly on the subject of racial and gender minorities, Freemasonry had all the common failings of eighteenth, nineteenth and twentieth century Western civilization. Simple twists of historical fate mixed with racism meant that at several times in our history, black men in America were kept from joining Masonic Lodges.

This led to the creation of Prince Hall Masonry, which catered almost exclusively to African Americans. While racial relations have greatly improved in the past four decades, diversity, particularly racial, can at times be an issue in our Lodge rooms. Several southern jurisdictions still refuse to interact in any way with Prince Hall Masons. Many of those same Lodges still refuse to accept African Americans into the Fraternity.

A *New York Times* article written in 2009 highlights this phenomenon, describing an incident when a young black Master Mason attended the annual meeting of the Grand Lodge of Georgia. Even in 2009, his attendance in and of itself was enough to provoke tongue wagging all over the state.

In an additional area related to inclusion and diversity, at the time this book was being written, two southern Grand Lodges issued edicts declaring homosexuality to be an immoral act under Masonic law. These edicts have the intent of barring openly gay men from becoming Masons and causing the expulsion of gay men who had already been initiated into the Fraternity.

Obviously, these behaviors are both disgraceful and abhorrent to the foundational ideas of Freemasonry. But even in jurisdictions that are faithful to the Masonic creed of accepting men of all races and religions, the majority of Lodges in this country consist of mostly white and Christian Brothers.

In contrast, millennials are the most diverse generation in American history.

• Forty percent of all millennials are racial minorities: 18 percent of the generation is Hispanic, 14 percent African American, 5 percent Asian, and 3 percent other.[40]

• Forty-three percent of all millennials are religious minorities: 35 percent consider themselves unaffiliated, 8 percent affiliate with faiths other than Christianity.[41]

• Seventy percent of all millennials believe that gay marriage is a civil right. This belief is unique in that it cuts across almost every race, religion, and locality.[42]

Millennial candidates will often not look or pray like the older members of your Lodge. Freemasonry has to be open to this possibility, because millennials expect it. Millennials were raised to believe in religious and racial diversity, and many of us were exposed to different cultures and faiths from a very early age. Intolerance towards racial, religious, and even gender minorities is abhorrent to millennials, as it should be for all Masons.

The Most Educated Generation in History: It is common knowledge that education opens the doorway to greater economic prosperity. Public education, and in particular a college education, has experienced increased accessibility in recent decades.

Each generation has increasingly availed themselves of these opportunities and become more educated than the last.

• 35 percent of generation Xers (The generation preceding millennials and following the baby boomers) received a college education.[43]

• As of 2013, an estimated 47 percent of millennials between the ages of twenty-five and thirty-four have received a postsecondary degree (associate's, bachelor's, or graduate degree). This percentage will only increase as younger millennials continue to graduate from institutions of higher learning.[44]

Millennials will want to continue to grow and learn as they become older and move further away from a traditional academic setting. Freemasonry has long been used as a vehicle for personal and spiritual growth and enlightenment. The Ritual gives us the examples of the perfect and imperfect ashlars as an example of how this might be done.

If you look toward the east in most Masonic Lodges you will see a podium often ascended to by three steps. You would also find two stones sitting on opposite sides of the steps. The Master of a Lodge sits on the highest step. To the right of the Master sits the "rough ashlar," an unworked piece of stone, meant to symbolize a man before he enters the Craft. If he scans his eyes to his extreme left he will encounter the "perfect ashlar," a piece of polished stone that is square, level, and plumb.

Metaphorically, Freemasonry is the path whereby a man can cross the gulf between the imperfect and perfect ashlar through personal growth and continuing education. The distance between the ashlars symbolizes a man's life. You attempt to move as close as you can to the perfect ashlar knowing full well you will never achieve perfection.

A young Ohio Mason recently shared this anecdote that highlights the millennial Mason's desire for education:

> *"We had a great discussion in my Lodge last night. Here's a summary:*
>
> *Young guys: We want education.*
>
> *Old guys: Back in my day, we were raising too many people to think about education.*
>
> *Young guys: Okay, but that's not the case now, so...education.*
>
> *Old guys: What do you want to know?*
>
> *Young guys: Uhh...*
>
> *Old guys: How can I help you when you don't know what you want?*
>
> *This same dialog happens a lot with us, and it tends to break down at that point. However, I wonder if what we really want is not for the old guys to grace us with answers, particularly because everyone's interpretation is different. Maybe what we really want is an environment where we can debate about what the questions should be."* [45]

A common expression used among Masons to describe the Fraternity to outsiders is that "Freemasonry is a peculiar system of morality, veiled in allegory and illustrated by symbols." Millennials will be intrigued by the challenge of unwrapping the many complicated layers of Masonic philosophy. If education is highlighted in the Craft, this will continue to be very attractive to younger members.

In a recent poll,

• 46 percent of millennial Masons surveyed proclaimed that they had joined Freemasonry because they were searching for either personal or spiritual knowledge. The words "esoteric" and "education" were used many times in the responses from this group. In contrast, only 29 percent of the respondents claimed to have joined Freemasonry to experience a brotherhood and universal fellowship regardless of one's age, creed, or race. Only 11 percent of the respondents were drawn to Freemasonry because of its history and only 12 percent were drawn to the Craft because of our charitable works or community activism.[46]

It is safe to infer that Lodges that guide its younger Brothers through varied and interesting educational opportunities will see millennial Masons come to the door in droves.

Interconnectivity and Technology: Millennials are the world's first digital natives. They are the only generation where the technological progress of the last twenty years has not been something they have needed to adjust to, rather for them it has always been a fact of life. Most millennials gather a significant amount of the information they process on a daily basis online, rather than through traditional print media.

Those organizations that do not have a significant presence on the Internet therefore, are working at a severe disadvantage when it comes to attracting millennial interest. Freemasonry has been slow to adjust to this change. Even today most Lodges do not have a web presence. If they do operate websites, many Lodges do little to maintain or update them. As a result, interested millennials have very few local avenues to express an interest in Freemasonry, unless they have a personal contact in a Lodge.

The Fraternity has expressed a general lack of interest and enthusiasm toward the digital revolution. Some members don't quite understand or trust the Internet. Some feel it is chaotic, hard to control, and is a venue whereby Masonic secrets can be easily divulged. This is reflected in draconian and archaic Grand Lodge edicts in several jurisdictions that regulate Freemasons who are active on social media.

A Grand Lodge in the Northeast, for example, forbids its members from contacting fellow Masons on social media platforms who reside outside of their jurisdiction unless they have received official permission from Grand Lodge. For digital natives, this thinking is backward and ineffectual. It stifles outside growth and hinders connections within the Fraternity across state lines in an age where technology can knit together Masons from all over the world.

Millennial Masons will eventually overpower this apathy. A contributor to *Forbes Magazine* summarizes,

"Millennials don't consume food, beverages, services, products or media in silence…. They review, blog and Tumblr, update Wikipedia entries and post YouTube, Vine and Instagram videos. Often these posts concern their consumption activities, interests and aspirations."[47]

Millennial Masons have begun to write Masonic blogs, create Facebook pages, and operate online podcasts and magazines. In fact, the millennial Mason's greatest contribution to Freemasonry, in the short term, might be bringing the digital revolution to the Craft.

Spirituality: Millennials are the first generation in modern American history where almost half of the population describe themselves as more spiritual than religious. This was in the context of discussing their views on the existence of a divine being and the true nature of the universe. What's the difference between spiritual and religious? And why does that matter to the Craft?

The English word "religion" has its roots in ancient Latin. *"Religio,"* a Latin word denoting "binding or obligation," eventually, through French influence, came to mean a belief in a particular system of faith, ritual, and worship in a particular superhuman controlling power, otherwise known as God. By definition, religion is an exclusive affair.

Whatever system you subscribe to offers a unique set of rituals and beliefs that provides some salvation from the maladies of the world. Often the inclusive words of the founders of these systems gave way to the interpretations of lesser men who used the demonization of other faiths as a tool in the furtherance of theirs.

Religious strife and intolerance has claimed the lives of millions throughout human history.

Though Freemasonry does possess a particular system of rituals and requires a belief in a supreme being, it is not a religion.

The only obligation demanded in Freemasonry is to your Brothers, widows, and orphans, in the eyes of God, but not to Him.

Freemasonry, while having its membership consist of mostly traditional, god-fearing men of all religious persuasions, has also been a haven for deists, agnostics, and other unorthodox religious beliefs.

Millennials are the least likely of any American generation to patronize organized religious institutions with their time, money, or beliefs.

• Sixty percent of millennials do not attend religious services on a regular basis.[48]

• In a country demographically dominated by Christianity, only 15 percent of millennials hold beliefs consistent with the Christian dogma.[49]

• Thirty-five percent of millennials have chosen to be unaffiliated with any religion. By comparison, only 15 percent of boomers are unaffiliated.[50]

By these metrics, millennials would seem to be some of the most unfit candidates to enter Lodge rooms as candidates, as a belief in a supreme being is one of the few requirements needed to begin a Masonic journey. But I would argue that it is actually quite the opposite. One of Freemasonry's greatest attributes is its insistence on a nonsectarian model and its emphasis on striving for personal growth and spiritual knowledge. Much of what drives millennial dissatisfaction with modern organized religions is their insistence on the exclusive nature of salvation. Almost all organized religions essentially imply or outright state that only they possess the correct route to spiritual fulfillment. Amongst millennials there is also an increasingly popular perception that organized religions are more interested in power and material gain than peace on earth and goodwill toward men.

Millennials explore their spirituality outside the confines of traditional religion.

• Forty-eight percent of millennials pray once week.[51]

• Seventy-two percent believe that God is a real being as opposed to an idea or a metaphor.[52]

• Seventy-five percent of millennials describe themselves as spiritual instead of religious.[53]

Though clergymen of all religions may bemoan this statistic, it could be a boon for Freemasonry as millennials enter our Lodges seeking an answer to this spiritual gap in their lives. This transition from Masonry as we currently understand it and this new concept of the Fraternity was explained quite nicely by this Millennial Brother from Ohio:

"The Ritual is sacred, we should treat it as such...silence and solemnity. Dim lights. Candles. This all fosters a meditative atmosphere that is sorely lacking from the world and which, when present, can make the Lodge all that it can be....If there is one thing, I think, the Ritual tells us, it's "Think, damn you!" And when you start doing that and thinking about what the Ritual means, you realize we are not a social club."[54]

Charitable Work: Millennials are often labeled as selfish. I believe that is an unfair characterization:

• Seventy-seven percent of millennials are motivated to serve others.[55]

• Eighty-seven percent of employed millennials gave more than one hundred dollars to charity in 2013.[56]

Millennials are changing the industry of charity, like every other facet of American culture they interact with. They are unlikely to donate to large, faceless charitable groups out of a lack of trust that those groups will actually spend their donation on the charitable causes they fight for.

Instead of donating, millennials want to invest, and see demonstrably what good their money has done for the world. This is part of the reason online crowd funding and charitable giving websites like Kickstarter and GoFundMe have become so popular.

Millennials are able to invest in projects they find worthwhile directly, and if the project is successful, they receive some form of reward depending on the amount of money they originally invested.

As discussed, most Lodges in the United States already put much of their focus into charitable works.

In some ways Lodge charity projects are ahead of the millennial curve. Many Lodges focus on small, local projects where Brothers can invest in people or organizations they already have a preexisting relationship with and can monitor what their efforts have accomplished.

While millennials may find charitable giving attractive, and even Masonic charitable giving attractive, it is usually not the primary attraction within Freemasonry. In a Masonic study consisting of millennial Masons: [57]

• Only 12 percent joined Freemasonry to perform charity work.

• Only 7 percent want to see charity emphasized more in their local Lodges.

• Only 15 percent of respondents named charity as their favorite aspect of the Craft.

Trust in Institutions: One reason millennials have begun to either create new institutions or change traditional ones has to do with their lack of trust in how the institutions currently run. This trust gap is important in understanding the role Freemasonry can play in the lives of millennials. Trust in institutions is an important part of civic engagement, and presently, trust is at an all-time low.

Several pillars of American society including businesses, charitable organizations, religious institutions, and government agencies are attempting to reinvent themselves in order to try and regain this trust.

The millennial generation is the first raised entirely in the suffocating cocoon of the twenty-four-hour mass media market. Both the Internet and the first twenty-four hour cable news networks were created in 1980, the same year the oldest millennials were born. As the apparatus of these two industries has continued to grow, they need to be fed more and more. What would have been considered "dirty laundry" thirty years ago is now considered journalistic gold. Each scandal leads to indictments, accusations, and reforms and more and more Americans disengaging from the pillars that have traditionally formed their communities.

Large and influential charities have been exposed as spending less of their money on the charitable causes that they represent and more on lavish offices, salaries, and expense accounts.

Molestation scandals, culture wars, and overseas religious strife have cast doubt on many of organized religions messages of peace, charity, and salvation. Millennials watched as big business and Wall Street banks tanked the economy in 2008 while their CEO's received golden parachutes. Meanwhile middle-income and poor Americans across the nation suffered. And when millennials overwhelmingly placed their hope in the transformative message of President Obama, ultimately their hopes began to feel misplaced and distrust in government has grown to an all-time high.

Each generation is said to have its defining events that leave a mark on their collective consciousness. These have been ours.

At the end of the day, millennials believe they can change the world, but they need an avenue that they can trust in order to do so. In this way our decline from the popular imagination is a benefit.

Freemasonry has not betrayed millennial trust yet. Within Freemasonry, millennials will find an organization of older mentors who can guide them regardless of race or religion through a lifetime of spiritual education and personal growth. The only thing that is missing from the modern Craft is a mechanism whereby millennials can begin to change the world.

Luckily, Freemasonry has a rich tradition of revolutionary action and thought. And while that tradition has faded from American Freemasonry, it is still very much relevant in global Freemasonry. Perhaps it is time for us to learn from our overseas brethren and restore this ancient paradigm to our Craft in America. This may be the most effective strategy for attracting and most importantly retaining this new breed of American men into our ranks.

MEN OF TYRE

FOR THOSE WHO FANCY THEMSELVES lifelong devotees to the Masonic arts, there are certain pilgrimages that almost all of us hope to make at some point in our short lives. Visiting the Grand Lodge of England, Mother Kilwinning Lodge in Scotland, and Solomon's Quarries in Jerusalem come to mind when envisioning a grand tour of Masonic sites across the globe. Often overlooked by globetrotting Masons, is Lebanon. It was known as Phoenicia in ancient times and was the homeland to our ancient Grand Master Hiram Abiff.

I made my own pilgrimage to this ancient land. In addition to serving as one of the backdrops to our Masonic origin story, there were other reasons for my visit. Demographically, the Lodges I visited in Lebanon are markedly younger than the typical American Lodge. The millennials are a much larger force in these Lodges. Why, I asked myself, are millennials drawn to Freemasonry in Lebanon? Lebanese Brothers face numerous social, religious, and sometimes life-threatening pressures. I believe this adversity has resulted in an institution that reflects the heritage and values that propelled international Freemasonry into the annals of history during the upheavals of the eighteenth and nineteenth centuries. These Brothers serve as modern-day testaments to the ability of Freemasonry to transcend sectarian barriers to create a brotherhood devoted to individual and societal improvement. I believe these traits will be critical to restoring and revitalizing the Craft in America so that the Fraternity remains relevant for the next generation of Masons.

It should be noted that whenever a westerner such as I travels to the East, it is very easy to fall into a pattern of Orientalist observation. By this I mean many of us, myself included, can unwittingly fall into patronizing depictions of cultures other than our own. Edward Said, in his groundbreaking book, *Orientalism*, coined the phrase to define the Western belief that there is a "basic distinction between East and West as the starting point for elaborate theories, epics, novels, social descriptions, and political accounts concerning the Orient, its people, customs, 'mind,' destiny and so on." In a country such as Lebanon, and in a city such as Beirut, it is especially easy to fall into this trap due to the sheer complexity of the country and its citizens. Knowing this, my observations about Beirut, Lebanon and the Fraternity therefore should be taken for what they are, the musings of an outsider looking in.

That being said, I believe the aspects that make Freemasonry in Lebanon special can be directly tied to the character and history of this country, dating back to the time of Solomon. By examining Lebanese history, we can draw parallels between the Lebanese Masonic experience, and our own.

Phoenicia, at the time of Hiram and Solomon, was a nexus of global trade, information, and technology. Multitudes of ethnic groups, states, and gods jostled for territory, prestige, and influence among the small coastal plain sandwiched between the Mediterranean Sea and the daunting Lebanon mountains. The native Canaanite religion was polytheistic and constantly evolving. Unlike their Jewish cousins to the south, who insisted on a monotheistic model, the Phoenician city-states easily adopted a multitude of foreign gods into their already crowded native pantheon. Temples to Zeus, Aphrodite, Bacchus, and various other Near Eastern deities shared the landscape with the native Phoenician gods. In some instances, such as the great temple in Baalbek, both the foreign and domestic deities shared the same space.

Baal, the storm god of the Phoenicians and patron god of Tyre reigned supreme in Phoenicia. The priests devoted to Baal are mentioned numerous times in the Hebrew Bible. Yahweh, the one supreme God of the Jewish people was worshiped in both Israel and Phoenicia, and conversely Baal was also worshiped in Israel, much to the consternation of Hebrew priests and prophets.

In fact, Hiram's example provides a striking illustration of religious toleration. As a man descended from both ethnicities, Hiram probably worshiped at the altars of both gods. But this peaceful coexistence was far from normal. The confrontation between the Hebrew prophet Elijah and the priests of Baal whereby Elijah orders the execution of a cadre of priests devoted to Baal, probably gives a more accurate depiction of the religious strife prevalent in both Israel and Phoenicia.

The worship of Baal and the other Phoenician gods spread across the Mediterranean in the hearts of Phoenician sailors and through the unmatched speed and durability of their legendary cedar ships. The cedar trees of Phoenicia were considered a prized commodity throughout the Mediterranean. The massive trees were known as some of the best material in the world for shipbuilding. Phoenician merchants sailed as far north as Great Britain, through the Straights of Gibraltar, to the western coast of Africa, and to the riches of India and Indonesia in these sturdy ships. Phoenicians established the storied and ancient cities of Carthage, Hippo, and Leptis Magna in Africa, and established settlements in Spain, France, Italy, and Greece, often astride the most important trade routes of the Mediterranean. The spoils of trade flowed into the coffers of Phoenician cities. Phoenician wine, unique and local purple dye (referred to as Tyrian purple), cedar wood, slaves, and glass flowed to

Greece and Egypt in return for gold and Egyptian cotton. From Spain, Sardinia, Africa, and India came precious silver, ebony, and ivory. When Hiram Abiff ventured from Tyre to Jerusalem, he left behind a city in a flourishing golden age of economic prosperity.

As a people devoted to trade over long distances, organization and the easy communication of information became a necessary skill for Phoenician traders. In response to this need, the Phoenicians developed the world's earliest written alphabet. Before this innovation, writing had been done in Egyptian hieroglyphics or Mesopotamian cuneiform that relied on crude drawings to represent complex concepts. This system was difficult to learn and was therefore restricted to the priestly and noble classes who had the time and resources for education. The Phoenician alphabet was the first writing system where one character had one sound attached to it, making it easy to learn and thereby relaxing the virtual monopoly the royalty and priests had on writing.

Using this new phonetic script, common people such as traders and farmers could use writing to disseminate information and organize their estates. The alphabet's simplicity also allowed the alphabet to be applied to multiple spoken languages. The written form of ancient Aramaic, Hebrew, Greek, Latin, and Arabic are all derived in some fashion from the Phoenician alphabet. Similarly, many modern languages and alphabets such as English, French, Spanish, Italian, modern Hebrew, and modern Arabic are all derived from this first Phoenician alphabet.

The more things change, the more they stay the same. While the characters have changed, the same motivations and central themes of the ancient Phoenician experience apply to modern Lebanon. As in ancient times, Lebanon is currently in the business of information.

While ancient Phoenicians pioneered early writing, modern Lebanese continue the literary tradition, hosting a litany of Arab, Eastern and Western print, online, television and radio outlets.

Beirut today is one of the intellectual nodes of modern Arab thought. Its democracy, while messy, dysfunctional, and in some ways abusive to its citizenry, still allows a freedom of expression and thought not commonly found in the rest of the Arab world.

While in competition with some of the Persian Gulf states, Beirut is still a beacon for literary-minded individuals from all over the Arab world. A traditional Arab expression, "Cairo writes, Beirut publishes and Baghdad reads"[58] is only partially true today. The recent rise of fundamentalism, war, and dictatorship has made it increasingly difficult for Baghdad to read and for Cairo to write, but Beirut, though often appearing at times on the precipice of chaos, has continued to publish.

While Phoenician ships no longer ply the trade routes between Phoenician colonies and the homeland, the vast Lebanese diaspora, constituting over fourteen million people in over forty-five countries, fulfills a similar role today, pumping an estimated 83 billion dollars into the Lebanese economy ever year.[59] Foreign remittances, tourism, banking, and other service-oriented products are to the modern Lebanese what Tyrian purple dye was to their ancient Phoenician ancestors.

Even the cedar tree, the lifeblood of Phoenician property, remains vital to modern Lebanon. While most of the country's forests have been destroyed, the cedar tree still is fundamental to the Lebanese spirit. It is displayed prominently on the nation's flag, coat of arms, airline, and armed forces. Many modern political parties incorporate it as a symbol in their logos, slogans, and literature. Modern Lebanon is still colloquially known as "the land of cedars."

And just as ancient Phoenicia was a hotbed of religious competition, strife, and syncretism, so too is modern Lebanon. While the ancient Greek, Egyptian, and Phoenician gods have disappeared, the population remains rigidly split along sectarian lines. There are eighteen official religions in the modern state of Lebanon. Shia Islam, Sunni Islam, Druze, Maronite Christianity, Greek Orthodox, Melkite Christianity, Protestants, Armenians, Syriacs, Copts, Chaldeans and Roman Catholics all tend their proverbial temple fires between the mountains and the sea. Even a small community of Jews keeps the belief in Yahweh alive on these ancient shores. Lebanon is one of the only countries in the world that practices confessionalist democracy. In this system, every ounce of civic power is distributed in a careful formula based on keeping the balance between so many diverse and quarrelsome groups. Each group is allocated its own courts and civil laws, as well as allocations in parliament. The president is required to be a Maronite, the prime minister a Sunni, and the speaker of the Parliament a Shi'a.

Lebanon's history in many ways mirrors the West. Both regions for many thousands of years have been characterized by religions, ethnicities and ideologies violently competing for adherents, territory and power. This power struggle encouraged the existence of Freemasonry. Its Universalist message allowed it to make a powerful impact and stake out significant positions in several Western nations. As the West has recently made progress in transcending these differences, Freemasonry's position has diminished. In Lebanon, a land of conservative clerics, Freemasonry continues to play a significant, albeit precarious, position in Lebanese society.

Presently there are eighteen Lodges in Lebanon, charted by the Grand Lodge of Scotland, New York, and the District of Columbia. Most of these Lodges are located in Lebanon's largest city, Beirut. Beirut is a physically beautiful city, perched on limestone cliffs overlooking the crystal blue Mediterranean Sea to the west and the Lebanon mountains to the east. But modern Beirut is a divided city in every way, divided by religion, ethnicity, financial status and utility access. It is a city where rich Christian neighborhoods, indistinguishable from neighborhoods in Rome or Paris, can coexist with refugee camps populated by the descendants of Palestinians fleeing the creation of Israel in 1948. It is a city where one can enjoy techno music and vodka sodas with the hopes of stumbling home with a scantily clad member of the opposite sex. But if you happen to take a wrong turn, you may find yourself in a neighborhood patrolled by a political party's paramilitary arm that is hostile to your religion or ethnic group. These differentiated neighborhoods act in a semi-autonomous fashion. Their residents are familiar and comfortable with each other, but find it difficult to interact in any meaningful way with the denizens of other neighborhoods with whom they usually do not share a first language, religion, or history. Despite the tensions, all of Lebanon's eighteen ethnic groups have a home in Beirut, making it a surprisingly tolerant and affable city.

Freemasonry first entered the Greater Syrian region in the 1860s. At that time Lebanon was a sleepy province of the Ottoman Empire, which was known as "the sick man of Europe" since the 1850s. The vast empire stretched from frozen Northern Europe to the deserts of Africa. While its territory and population were large, the empire was long past its golden age and was lagging far behind other European empires in almost every measurable category.

While the Europeans transitioned from agricultural economies to manufacturing and commercial systems, the Ottomans retained a traditional, agrarian economy. Ottoman exports consisted mostly of raw products for European consumption such as cotton, silk, and foodstuffs. Railways were built in the empire forty years after they had become a key cog in the European economy. Financed by European traders, the Ottoman railways often skipped interior provincial capitals or population centers, linking the coast to areas that manufactured products for the European market. Rising military and administration costs sent the empire into a spending spree that resulted in a debt equivalent to 10 percent of the empire's gross domestic product. The military, while well financed, was defeated by one European and rebel army after another, losing territory to European empires and allowing economically successful regions, such as the Balkans, to gain independence.

Beirut was one of the few Ottoman cities to experience an economic boom during these tumultuous times. Leveraging its close economic relationship with France, Beirut exploded from a small port of ten thousand people in 1860 to one of the largest trading entrepôts of the empire, numbering 116,000 citizens just fifty years later. The growing bourgeoisie of the Arab portion of the Ottoman Empire, Muslim, Jew, and Christian alike, were increasingly reform minded.

This cultural movement, coined *al Nahda*, Arabic for "awakening," argued for embracing Western modernism and merging that modernism with certain Islamic and Arab ideals. Al-Nahda began in Egypt but eventually spread to the bourgeoisie of the cosmopolitan cities of the Arab world, such as Baghdad, Damascus, Jaffa, and of course Beirut. When describing the men who endorsed the al-Nahda movement, a well-respected historian described them as "cosmopolitan but local, and pro-reform but neither anti state nor against community."[60] The spirit of al-Nahda was best encompassed by the lives of several philosophers who espoused this awakening in various parts of the empire. In Beirut, the most influential of these men was Butrus al-Bustani.

Born a Maronite Christian in the area surrounding Mount Lebanon, al-Bustani was exposed to numerous Western concepts and citizens while serving as an interpreter for the British armed forces and the American consulate. While educated in a religious setting, al-Bustani began to advocate for a secular identity for the Lebanese people after witnessing the sectarian bloodletting between all the religious groups around Mount Lebanon in 1860. He focused on the shared Arab language and culture that would bridge the gaps between the feuding religious sects.

Al-Bustani was able to adopt European concepts to the unique local culture of the Arab lands. For this he became known as "the father of the Arabic renaissance." Al-Bustani himself never joined Freemasonry, but many of his disciples flocked to the early Masonic Lodges being founded in Beirut. While originally founded and populated by European expatriates living in Beirut, Freemasonry quickly became a native institution in the city. Early modern Lodges in Beirut consisted mostly of traders and merchants, but included government employees, military personnel, landowners, teachers, doctors, lawyers, hotel managers, tailors, and journalists, as well as priests and imams.

The societal rifts in Ottoman Lebanon were vast. While individual improvement was the main reason to join Freemasonry, academic and Lebanese Freemasonry expert Dorothe Sommer wrote,

"It seems Lodges were built mainly to realize the hopes of members to reach out to the profane world.... the main topic engaging most of the men's minds concerned what the next day would bring and how they would be able to survive in a society in which rifts were becoming continuously more pronounced." [61]

As an outgrowth of Masonic philosophy, these Lodges served as a platform to increase inter religious tolerance and stability. Men of all religious persuasions were welcomed into Lodges.

As a result, Freemasonry was attacked on all sides by the entrenched religious institutions in Lebanon, both Christian and Muslim alike. The Masonic values of tolerance, internationalism, democracy, and egalitarianism caused nervous qualms in many conservative social and religious circles. These values made Masonic Lodges a welcome retreat for adherents of the al-Nahda movement, and in this way the Fraternity became involved in the reform movements of the late Ottoman Empire. As Sommer describes,

"While not complying with a specific political agenda, the Lodges in greater Syria were political insofar as they influenced relationships between men who were politically and or socio/culturally active." [62]

As you may recall, Lodges performed a similar function in the United States prior to the Morgan Affair. These Lebanese Brothers viewed their membership as a tool to end the sectarian conflict that so permeated their daily lives. If Lodges were able to increase their membership, then soon everybody would recognize that fighting over religious identities was futile; the only the way the land would survive in a coherent fashion was religious tolerance.

This is not just conjecture from the present. The Lebanese of that time period viewed the organization as a socio-cultural movement. In a series of letters between Lebanese Lodges in 1905, the purpose of Freemasonry in Lebanon was considered to be "generating social and moral evolution" while fighting for "peace, progress, and welfare," and was the focus of "intellectual and moral enlightenment, fighting ignorance, fanaticism, and atavistic egotism."[63] Unity through strength became the mantra of Lebanese Masons during this time.

After the final collapse of the increasingly weak Ottoman Empire, Beirut's all important European trading partner, France, imposed a twenty-year occupation on both Syria and Lebanon. After gaining independence in 1943, Lebanon enjoyed a period of political stability. Beirut's position as a, regional center of finance and free trade fueled the nation's wealth. At the height of this prosperity, between 1958 and 1966, Beirut became known as "the Paris of the Middle East." It was lauded for its world-class cuisine, its reputation as a popular tourism destination, its fascinating blend of Parisian and Ottoman architecture, and its wealth and stability.

But in the land of Lebanon, stability does not last long amid the crowded landscape. Branded in the West as a "Middle Eastern Switzerland" due to its political neutrality, mountainous terrain and economic wealth, the United States and Europe misunderstood the simmering tensions among the multitudes of Lebanon's ethnic groups.

The Middle Eastern wars between Israel and its neighbors brought Palestinian refugees fleeing north to escape the Israeli annexation of the West Bank and Gaza. Lebanon, already divided among so many ethnic and religious groups, was now charged with housing over four hundred thousand Palestinian refugees. In a country so dominated by the constant balancing of ethnic and religious groups, the introduction of so many new parties into the equation created a constitutional crisis.

Society was able to muddle through for almost a decade marked by an increase in distrust and violent behavior. Ethnic groups on all sides started to create militia to defend themselves and their neighborhoods against others. The government and the military began to divide along similar lines. On April 13, 1975, a running street battle began, pitting the Palestinian Liberation Organization (PLO) and the Maronite Christian militia, colloquially known as the "Phalange," against each other. Lebanon would not know peace for the next seventeen years.

The country devolved into a sectarian bloodletting, pitting ever-changing loose alliances of militia groups against one another. Outside powers quickly became involved for both humanitarian and self-serving reasons. Israel invaded in 1982, forming an alliance with the Christian militia against the PLO, in the hope of stopping Palestinian attacks against northern Israel.

An international force of Italians, British, French, and Americans was inserted into the country in an effort to stop the bloodletting, but was withdrawn after only two years due to constant harassment by multiple parties culminating in Hezbollah bombing a US Marine barracks, killing over three hundred American and French servicemen.

Neighboring Syria occupied varying amounts of Lebanese territory until 2005. At that point, a groundswell of popular support and protests forced the occupying army to finally leave Lebanon, unoccupied by a foreign power for the first time since 1982.

The country's infrastructure was devastated and its internal fraternal ties with one another were severed after almost 120,000 men women, and children perished and over one million of their countrymen had fled abroad to escape the violence.

In the midst of this sectarian bloodletting of the civil war, the tolerance of Freemasonry stood no chance. Like candles being extinguished, the light of the Masonic Lodges flickered out of existence one by one. Freemasonry in Lebanon would not be formally reconstituted until the late 1980s when the civil war was coming to an end.

Though Lebanon had experienced a decade of stability and economic growth after the war, at the time of my visit in 2015 the country seemed poised on the precipice of being once again swallowed into the abyss of its past chaos. The vicious civil war in neighboring Syria had caused over one million Syrian refugees to flood into Lebanon. In a country of only four million, which had been so carefully calibrated upon religious and ethnic populations and simultaneously recovering from its own civil war, this influx of desperate people stretched every portion of Lebanese society to the breaking point. Public utilities such as cell phone service, water delivery, electricity, and garbage collection groaned under the added pressure. Paralyzed by sectarian politics, the political elite found itself unable to provide direction in the crisis. Meanwhile across the mountainous border, the Sunni terrorist organization, ISIS, best known in the West for its brutal war crimes against Muslims and Christians alike, probed the nation's defenses searching for signs of weakness, hoping to continue its expansion across the Middle East and Africa. Shortly before my arrival, the utility crisis finally came to a boil. Beirut's main landfill reached capacity and, without a quick solution, trash began to fill the streets of Beirut, creating a public health crisis that lead to sometimes violent protests in the center of the city.

In my travels through Beirut I met many extraordinary Masons who were able to provide me with much valuable insight into both Lebanese Freemasonry and Lebanese society as a whole. I would love to introduce them and explain how they came to the Fraternity to add a personal touch to this otherwise impersonal reflection on the Lebanese Craft. Unfortunately, I cannot. As I already mentioned, both the Christian and Muslim establishment in Lebanon loathe Freemasonry. In a religious nation, these voices carry weight, and have managed to turn much of the population against the Craft. Muslim clerics preach that Freemasonry is a Zionist conspiracy used as a tool to subvert traditional Muslim society. Christian clerics have long viewed Freemasonry as antithetical to Christianity and equally as subversive. As such, threats to Freemasons in Lebanon vary in intensity, but never disappear entirely. In the past, various militia groups and the Syrian secret police threatened Freemasons and their families with death. Today, members feel less physically threatened, but still face being ostracized by both friends and family members if their membership is divulged to the wrong person. Lodges meet in hidden rooms in out-of-the-way and unmarked industrial settings to avoid prying eyes. For these reasons, revealing any information about who these Brothers are, or where they meet would be a grave mistake on my part.

Lebanese Brothers today must navigate a society that institutionalizes religious and ethnic separatism. Our ancient brethren in the West also negotiated a similar landscape in the eighteenth and nineteenth centuries. While Lebanese Lodges organize themselves along linguistic lines to reflect the unique circumstances of life in modern Lebanon, they also have a clear and direct mission to transcend the numerous barriers in Lebanon that separate the eighteen recognized groups from one another. In contrast to the sectarian separation of the city, in Lebanese Lodges one can find Maronite Christians, Catholics, Protestants, Muslims (both Shia and Sunni), Druze, Armenians, and Agnostics in the same Lodge room. On their altars you will find both the Koran and the Bible side by side. In this divided country, this one simple image is intensely beautiful.

Lebanese Freemasons are a special breed and they stand out among the general populace. Although there are only six hundred Freemasons in the entire country, they are both young (the average age of a Lebanese Mason is thirty-five) and enthusiastic. Many are university educated. They are comfortable moving between different sectarian groups and they are accustomed to traveling abroad for business and pleasure. Many of these Brothers do not remember Lebanese Freemasonry before the civil war, and if they do, they do not appear to hold the old grievances from the conflict. In speaking with them, I could not help but wonder if these new Brothers are the future leaders of this country. After they have inculcated the tenants of the Fraternity, will they bring them to their country just as a generation of American Brothers brought the tenets of this Craft to ours? It is all speculation now, but I am optimistic for the future of these Brothers and their country.

Lebanese Freemasonry is not necessarily a model for North American Masonry. In fact, I think most of the Lebanese Brothers would laugh if I made that claim. But there is a lesson to be derived from their experience. In both Lebanon and North America, the ideals of Freemasonry have inspired men to lead nations and peoples towards revolutionary socio-economic change. This revolutionary change disappeared in both nations and within the Masonic culture, but for very different reasons. Lebanese Freemasonry almost entirely ceased to exist as an organization amid the hellish din of a twenty-year civil war. In American Freemasonry, this revolutionary impulse was slowly bled out of the Craft by men who were simply looking for a different experience. Now, in Lebanon, Freemasonry has returned, and I am optimistic that the young men I encountered there have already begun the slow and arduous work towards peace and understanding in Lebanon, taking the tenets of Freemasonry into their communities in an attempt to improve their society. It is high time for us in North America to begin the restoration work needed so that we may empower our members to go out and do the same. The more things change, the more they stay the same.

MILLENNIAL
LODGE #1

W HAT WOULD A LODGE THAT ATTRACTS and retains millennial Brothers feel like? This chapter turns theory into practice for many of the concepts we have explored in earlier chapters.

The ability to have vibrant and open debate on the philosophical underpinnings that make up our society was, in the past, an essential component of Masonry. It should be so once again in the modern era.

Lodges in the eighteenth and nineteenth centuries were great forums for ideas and discussions. But, gradually, the prohibition on "politics" has created an artificial barrier between Lodges and the civic community. These barriers need to be reduced, so that Masonry can once again exemplify Joseph Fort Newton's belief that Masonry should act as a "ministry to the individual, and through the individual to society and the state." To be clear, I am not endorsing the idea of Lodges engaging in political activities.

But in the modern age, these artificial barriers have effectively denied millennial Masons a path whereby they feel empowered to change their communities, societies, and nations for the better. In the present, Masonry stands at the crossroads of a unique opportunity as the largest generation in American history comes of age. The Observance Movement, through its commitment to restoring a sense of awe to our ceremonies, excellence in Ritual, exclusivity in membership, and its insistence on solemnity, philosophical thought, and the sacred space of the Lodge room, has dramatically assisted interested Brothers in reclaiming the spiritual aspects of the Craft.

On top of this positive development, we can now begin the reclamation of Masonry as the socio-cultural movement that it was, should be, and I hope will become again. The following are ways in which Lodges may begin to break down those barriers. Again, these are not activities that endorse engaging in political activities. They will simply make it easier for Lodges to be both intellectually consistent, and I hope inspire Masons to return to their communities to advocate and fight for Masonic traditions and values, giving Masons the capability of once again changing our world.

Egalitarianism and Universal Brotherhood

Egalitarianism is a social philosophy that advocates the removal of inequalities among people. In Masonic Lodges, during the Second Degree, Masons are taught that even "men on the lowest spoke of fortune's wheel may be entitled to the same respect and dignity as a man lucky enough to have acquired riches." New York Ritual proudly proclaims that "the high, the low, the rich, the poor may meet with one common purpose." While a Masonic Lodge contains several raised platforms, Lodges generally end their meetings with no Brother standing higher than the other, to remind us that regardless of rank or station in the Fraternity or outside of it, we are all equal before the Great Architect of the Universe.

Reduced Emphasis on Nationalism: In Millennial Lodge #1 Brothers can expect not to see any national flag or recite any pledge of allegiance to a civil authority.

One of the most divisive and yet artificial dividers of men that has ever been conceived is the concept of nationality. It is often said that more men have been killed in the name of God than for any other motivation. If that is true, then the countless lives lost for the sake of national borders cannot be far behind. Some of Freemasonry's most poignant stories of brotherhood consist of men crossing contentious national lines in the midst of armed conflict to provide aid, comfort, and safety to one another.

In American Freemasonry, many of these stories are set during the Civil War, when our nation ripped itself apart and Brothers, both in Masonry and in blood, launched themselves at one another with startling cruelty and depravity. But amid the bloodletting, the ties of Masonic fellowship oftentimes remained unbroken.

These examples of Masonic courage are widely celebrated, as they should be. And yet in recent times, Masonry has done a disservice to these Brothers by paying fealty to the very thing that they stood against. In many jurisdictions not only is the American flag displayed in Lodge rooms, but also in some instances it is mandated that the Brothers recite the Pledge of Allegiance during every Lodge meeting. We rightly celebrate Masonry's universality. Yet, in the sanctum sanctorum of Masonry's quest to transcend man-made constructs such as race and nationality, we choose to pay homage to one of the very things that drives Brothers into disharmony.

This was not always so. In 1963, at the heart of America's Cold War with the Soviet Union, the Grand Lodge of West Virginia denounced this practice, stating,

> *"Although the American flag may be displayed in our Lodge halls, no ceremony with respect to it and no pledge of allegiance are permitted. To do otherwise in our judgment violates the principles of universality to which we are committed by our ritual."* [64]

An Emphasis on Religious Plurality: In Millennial Lodge #1 Brothers can expect to see many different volumes of sacred law, open on the altar of Freemasonry.

For most of American history, the Fraternity of Freemasonry has consisted predominantly of Christian men. Therefore, while men of other faiths and ideologies have been permitted to take their Masonic obligation on any volume of sacred law they chose, the Christian Bible is often the only holy book that can be found on a Lodge's altar. Adding a Koran, Torah, or any other volume of sacred law shows both a desire to learn from other religious traditions and an effort to salute the underpinning universal tenets that can be found in every religious text. Thereby once again highlighting the ability of the Fraternity to unite diverse groups of men. Adding another volume of sacred law also symbolizes recognition that a growing number of millennial Masons are identifying their spirituality in other ways than those traditionally associated with the Fraternity.

Removing Barriers to Brotherhood: In Millennial Lodge #1 Brothers can expect to enjoy a fraternal relationship with a sister Lodge in another nation.

After removing parochial national flags and anthems from our Lodge rooms, it is imperative we practice what we preach and venture across national borders in search of brotherhood. Over fifteen American jurisdictions border another nation. Lodges will be encouraged to visit yearly with one another and establish a fraternal relationship regardless of differences of race, language, or national affiliation. For jurisdictions that are not located within close proximity of a border, modern technology has made it convenient for Lodges to reach out to brethren all over the world. For instance, a Lodge in California has managed to kindle and maintain a relationship with a Lodge in Germany, where papers are sent back and forth via e-mail, translated, and read aloud in Lodge.

In fact, with modern technology, it's certainly feasible through video conferencing to have joint Lodge meetings with any Lodge throughout the world that possesses the necessary technological capabilities.

The Destruction of Institutional Racism and Homophobia: In Millennial Lodge #1 Brothers can expect to encounter men of all races, cultures, faiths, and sexual persuasions.

Grand Lodges that still refuse to recognize Prince Hall Masonry and have issued edicts regulating the sexuality of its members must begin the work necessary toward mending the centuries-long divide between them.

There are both philosophic and pragmatic reasons for this. Philosophically, while these jurisdictions insist their denial of amity is based on Prince Hall's supposed "irregularity," it appears to millennials as old-fashioned racism. And, of course, this type of behavior is in violation of every tenet of Masonry. Pragmatically, these Lodges will not be able to make a claim on the 40 percent of millennials that are nonwhite, and quite possibly the other 60 percent who have been raised since birth to abhor this type of behavior. Similarly with over 70 percent of millennials in support of gay unions, they will be hesitant to join an organization that espouses universal equality while barring large segments of the population from their Lodge rooms.

All of these preceding measures could be enacted with the goal of inspiring Masons to advocate for an elimination of racism, the elimination of hostile borders while simultaneously championing religious toleration, and world peace.

This promise of equality, brotherly love, and peace is all the more pertinent for twenty-first century America. Who among us can say this country has no more work to do when it comes to peaceful discourse between the multitudes of groups that inhabit this land? The events in Ferguson, Baltimore, and Staten Island prove that increased dialogue is needed and Masons could be at the forefront of the continuing work that is required to stitch this country together.

As Joseph Salem, an Israeli Freemason wrote,

"The problem before the world is the problem of living together. It is made acute by the fact that the huge world of ancient times, with its vast separating distances, has vanished, and in its place we have a little world, shriveled to the size of a neighborhood—noisy, gossipy, and often disagreeable. Drawn together, jammed together, we must learn to live together. "Thou shall love thy neighbor as thyself." This is the Commandment to which Freemasonry dedicated itself, to establish Brotherhood among men so they can live in peace with each other in this world. The struggle of Freemasonry is the struggle of the human race against tyranny and oppression. From the beginning, Freemasonry has realized that religion, tradition, and habits of life can divide the peoples of the world into hostile camps. Freemasonry takes no part in these quarrels, rather it provides a common meeting ground where all men can meet on the level." [65]

Democratic Values

Democracy is the control of an organization or state by the majority of its members.

Since its early genesis in medieval stone guilds, a form of rough democracy has always governed Masonry. While the Master of a Lodge has a wide array of almost dictatorial powers, both he and his officers are still required to be voted into office and both Master and officers are forced to abdicate these positions of power once their term has come to a close. In the eighteenth century, in many parts of the world, voting in the officer line was the only experience in democracy that citizens were ever able to exercise. In conjunction with this, since Lodges provided a safe environment to discuss radical and sometimes revolutionary philosophies, Lodges also became the only place for men to exercise freedom of speech or freedom of conscience.

In the modern day, most Lodges do not debate, discuss, or even truly elect its officer line. The advocates of the Observance Movement have already given lengthy expositions on the merit of electing an officer line, but even more important is a return to debating important philosophical and moral issues. I believe this is a useful endeavor for Lodge programming, Masonic education, and most important, individual advocacy.

An Assembly of Ideas: In Millennial Lodge #1, in every meeting, Brothers can expect to actively engage in the debate of important philosophical concepts and can expect to be trained in the finer points of civic engagement such as civil disagreement, cogent arguing, leadership skills, and how to properly advocate for your ideals.

In the eighteenth and nineteenth centuries, Masonic Lodges were veritable training grounds for the democratic civil society that replaced monarchial courts after the age of democratic revolutions.

Freemasons elected their officers, freely and civilly discussed weighty ideological topics, and developed leadership skills all by just attending Lodge. This was unique because many of these activities, such as elections and free debate, could only be found in Masonic Lodge rooms at that time. Being a good citizen of their Lodge actively prepared those Brothers to be good citizens in a greater society.

Today, this concept has all but vanished from our Lodges. The Grand Lodge of Nebraska has recently adopted a so-called Socrates Café programming for Lodges. It was born out of a Brother asking himself the question, "What did early Lodges discuss before history and famous past Masons existed?"[66] This program was created in the hope that Lodges would once again become "places of great learning and discussion about topics of great importance to all men in an atmosphere of safety and cooperation." Brothers debate topics using the liberal arts and the sciences of grammar, rhetoric, and logic. They are challenged intellectually, required to explain their world view and defend any arguments put forth.

True Elections for Officers: In Millennial Lodge #1, the direction of the Lodge will be decided in a transparent and respectful election.

I have described how many progressive line systems operate in Masonic Lodges and how the Observance Movement has already voiced its concerns regarding this practice. But since I believe this is one of the most entrenched customs in North American

Freemasonry, I believe it is appropriate to raise the issue once more. Of course every Lodge is different, and many Lodges have adopted the progressive line out of necessity due to a lack of numbers or a belief that the progressive line effectively trains officers on their way to the Masters chair. There is also a belief that holding true elections will result in electioneering and ultimately create disharmony in the Lodge.

While progressive lines in healthy Lodges do create a sense of predictability and consistency while providing on-the-job training to officer candidates, I also believe that not only is that outcome far from the norm, but it is directly opposed to the original intent of Masonic belief.

At the time of the modern Fraternity's founding, a version of what we would call a progressive line system existed all around the world in the form of Monarchical succession. This system allowed many unqualified and uneducated men and women to ascend their thrones and wreak havoc among their citizenry.

Freemasons, committed to enlightenment principles, chose the radical route of electing its leaders. While electioneering and improper decorum can be, and has, been a problem in the past, the progressive line system in unhealthy Lodges has bred systematic nepotism, stifled innovation and undercuts the Fraternity's proud tradition of democratic values.

Every Brother should have a say in the direction of his lodge. A system can be designed to prevent electioneering and provide a forum for a respectful, open competition of ideas and philosophies, creating a more inclusive atmosphere in Lodge and a sense that all members have a stake and say in the Lodge's success or failure.

Morality

Morality is a particular system of values and principles of conduct, especially one held by a specified person or society. What constitutes correct moral behavior is often tied to what belief system or society in which you find yourself immersed. Islamic morality is very different from Jewish morality. American morality is very different from Chinese morality. Masonry is often described as a "peculiar system of morality, veiled in allegory, illustrated by symbols."

In eighteenth century American Lodges, Freemasonry viewed itself as a moral university for the common man, free of the superfluities of religion or government. This was important to our fledgling democracy. Before the revolution, only a small group of men, often residing across the ocean, were entitled to make decisions for the masses. After the revolution, at least in theory, every American male citizen was required to take an active part in governing the country. Without moral training, what stops men from using this new found power for personal gain? As Brother Theodore Roosevelt once said,

"To educate a man in mind and not in morals is to educate a menace to society."[67]

Masonic morality is a fairly simple ideology. It is explained through the various Degrees by adopting the Operative Masons working tools and metaphorically denoting each tool as a lesson for a Mason's life. What has always made Masonic morality attractive is that it manages to be both simple and uncontroversial. It is a synthesis of the most pure and foundational pieces of the Abrahamic religions and Western culture, while also being open to lessons from other traditions. Its simplicity keeps it free of corruption and its inclusiveness allows for flexibility within different traditions. The lessons of the working tools are universal to Masons wherever they may reside:

- The Compass teaches Masons to contain their desires through self-restraint and control.

- The Level reminds Masons that every man is traveling on a similar path that ultimately ends in death, that no man can escape it, and as such in death we are equal, therefore so shall we be in life.

- The twenty-four inch gauge teaches Masons to achieve balance in their lives by dividing their time in three equal parts dedicated to work, rest, and relief of our fellow man.

- The Gavel, used by Operative Masons to shear off the rough edges of stones, admonishes Masons to reject immorality and become men of character and honor.

- The Trowel, used by operative Masons to smooth cement, reminds Masons that brotherly love and affection is the cement that "unites us into one sacred band, or society of friends and Brothers, among whom no contention should ever exist."

- The Plumb Line and the Square serve as reminders to Brothers that they should always act upright, square their actions and always refer back to the working tools when in a moral quandary.

Masonic morality therefore is really quite simple and uncontroversial.

A Mason should
- practice self-control;
- believe that since all men are mortal, we are all equal;
- work towards achieving balance in his life, spending his

day at various times working, resting, and devoting a part of every day to some form of philanthropy;

- actively try to identify his vices and do his best to combat them; and always remember that his fellow Masons are his Brothers and that their bond is stronger than any petty argument or disagreement he may have with another.

Collective Focus on Moral Training: In Millennial Lodge #1 Brothers can expect regular opportunities for reflection on their personal journeys toward the perfect ashlar.

This code of morality is the basis for that old trope that Masonry "makes good men better". And yet, very rarely in the course of a Masonic life is one questioned about this journey. It is often assumed that just by completing Masonry's initiatic experience and being an active Lodge member, you will become a better, more moral man.

The Lodge experience that I envision would begin with a young millennial searching for something more out of his life.

This millennial would be simultaneously disillusioned with the major institutions and greater society that surround him, and be relentlessly optimistic about his future. The millennial has heard of Freemasonry most likely through some popular culture medium that still, after three hundred years, finds itself fascinated by the idea of Freemasonry. This will mean that he already possess some preconceptions and expectations of the Craft. Like many of his generation, once he has an interest, the very first place he will turn to is the Internet. After sifting through the millions of webpages containing both useful information and misinformation, he will finally find the sleek and modern website of his local Lodge that will detail our Masonic ideals, our location, and include a pathway for this young man to contact the Lodge. Due to our reduced numbers, millennials will oftentimes not have access to the Fraternity through the time-tested manner of referrals, therefore making this last point crucial to our outreach efforts.

Once contact has been made, Lodges will guard their doors very closely. This millennial is trying to join an elite and exclusive organization. He will feel there is a wide gulf between the Lodge and himself, and he must do his utmost to close that gap through hard work and study. The Lodge will very slowly bring this potential candidate into the fold, having several meetings to determine whether this young man is worthy of being a Mason. The Lodge will also determine how well he fits into the Lodge's culture and whether he is joining the Craft for the appropriate reasons. This process would take several months and involve multiple Brothers. This would all occur before the candidate is even allowed to ask for a petition. Again, the candidate should not feel as if we are desperate for any warm body. The idea that he may be denied entry is both a powerful motivational tool for him and a way for us to insulate Freemasonry from the unmotivated, unserious, and unworthy.

Once this young man enters the Degree process, the ritualistic and solemn environment of a Masonic Lodge will awe him. This will most likely be his first encounter with this type of sacred atmosphere and if the Degrees are performed to a high standard, this experience will profoundly change his life. After his First Degree, it is time for this millennial to go back to work. He has been lucky enough to make it this far, but now it is time to study.

With the help of an older mentor, our young millennial Mason will study for months to pass proficiency for his Second and Third Degrees. Failure to do so will result in being held back a year or even dismissal from the Degree process. Through this time, our young millennial candidate will be educated in the symbolism of the Craft, the history of his Lodge, and, most importantly, the bond with a designated mentor and the other members of his Lodge.

By the time he is raised, this millennial Mason will not only feel a sense of accomplishment, having been accepted into his Lodge and having worked to pass all the necessary tests to join this elite group, but also truly recognize that he has entered into a spiritual band of Brothers. After his raising, our millennial Brother will have entered a Lodge dedicated to spirituality; solemnity; moral education; instruction in egalitarianism; schooling in rhetoric, logic, and grammar; an emphasis on scholarship; and a firm belief that Masonry can change the world, and his Lodge encourages its members to go out and do just that.

CONCLUSION

I WILL END THIS PIECE OF MASONIC education with a simple declaration of my intent.

I do not believe that one style or genre of Masonry is any better than the other. Masonry can mean many things to many people, and what Masonry means to you and your Brothers at your local Lodge should be based entirely on what the majority of your members want out of their Masonic experience.

This book is solely my opinion. I have tried to construct a cogent argument based on my understanding of Masonic history, Masonic philosophy, the millennial generation, and both my personal Masonic experience and the experiences of those around me. I have come to these conclusions after much research and thought, and whether they are "correct" or not I will leave for you to judge.

I will conclude this book with the following scene, a brief imagining of how one moment of my ideal "Millennial Lodge" might look and sound. It is my belief that if we want to take advantage of this historic opportunity and simultaneously reclaim a portion of our joint Masonic heritage, the following may be a way forward for the Craft as a whole, and your Lodge in particular.

Imagine yourself in the interior of a Masonic Lodge. The room is an ornate, yet intimate structure, softly lit by candlelight. On each side of the room a number of Brothers place themselves deliberately in front of white pedestals. Adorning each pedestal is a solitary candle and several matches. The Brothers in Millennial Lodge #1 are practiced and prepared for lively debate and the exchange of important ideas. The officers have structured roles and prepare for these thoroughly. The new brethren are slowly brought along by their mentors to participate in Lodge discussion.

At the rap of a gavel, the Worshipful Master in the East rises and begins to speak:

WM: Brethren, it is time to begin this evening's quest for knowledge, wisdom, and Masonic light.   One of the most vexing questions that has plagued humanity since our inception is the quandary of "free will."

Do we truly have control over our actions?   And if so, to what degree?   Is there a divine plan that governs our every motion?   And if so, how responsible are we for our own actions?   Our fellow Brother and esteemed philosopher, Rene Descartes, defined free will as having the ability to freely choose any path, the soul and the brain in conjunction allowing us to take any trail we choose.

Brother Descarte's theory was so influential that many in society subscribe to this belief in some fashion or another.   This question predates ancient Greek philosophy, and, make no mistake, we will not find an answer here today.   But, we will further our understanding of the universe that surrounds us, shining some light where before there was only darkness.   I will note that this discussion, as always, has implications for us today as we look at our decisions day to day and the choices we make as we work toward becoming better men and Masons.

During this monologue, both the Senior and Junior Warden, in a preordained fashion, will have lit their candles, symbolizing their willingness to speak on this topic. The Worshipful Master addresses the Senior Warden:

WM: Senior Warden.

SW: Thank you, Worshipful Master. You are correct in pointing out the longevity of this perplexing philosophical debate. The ancient Greek philosophers debated this relentlessly. Aristotle, the famous philosopher and tutor to Alexander the Great, believed that events are not determined by prior events, allowing for a form of chance and randomness in the universe. Other ancient philosophers argued for a form of determinism, arguing that since human beings are essentially made of atoms, and atoms follow natural laws, that human beings, as well, simply follow the natural laws of the universe.

You would think, in the past two thousand years, and with all the scientific advancements we have made, we would have achieved some clarity on this debate. Frankly, we have not. The modern debate is quite similar to the ancient one. Some modern philosophers interpret the Heisenberg Principle, which shows that one cannot measure the behavior of quantum particles without inherently changing their behavior as proof that the natural laws that govern the smallest molecules are not unbreakable. Otherwise, molecules would not change behavior when observed. Therefore some form of free will, or at least ambiguity or chance, must exist.

As for myself, I find myself agreeing that humanity must possess some form of free will. Of course there are degrees of freedom. None of us is truly free, nor are we wholly in bondage either. But our bondage is not based on any natural laws of the universe, but is based on laws of our own design. Our various societal and personal moralities subjugate the otherwise free choices we might make. I look forward to discussing this further with the brethren. Thank you Worshipful Master.

Throughout the Lodge room, various Brothers have begun to light their candles, signifying their desire to speak on the topic. The Worshipful Master next addresses the Junior Warden, who is prepared to present the other side of the issue:

WM: Junior Warden.

JW: Thank you, Worshipful Master. I would like to respectfully disagree with my Brother in the West. Though he made many excellent points on this subject, I would like to focus on what the Senior Warden calls "natural law." There is no definition of what constitutes natural law. Believing in natural law is to believe that there is a system of right or justice that is common to all man and derived from nature or divinity, as opposed to the rules of society. As he already described, the Senior Warden believes that most of a man's decisions are inherently influenced by the society that surrounds him, but nevertheless, the final decisions come from the man himself.

I, on the other hand, believe that there is such a thing as "natural law", and it is from natural law that societal law derives. As such, all human decision-making can be traced back to this more ancient natural law. If we are only following this natural law handed down to us from the universe, or some Grand Architect of the Universe, free will cannot exist. I look forward to discussing this further with the brethren. Thank you, Worshipful Master.

More and more Brothers have now begun to light their candles, and while the Senior Warden has also relit his flame to continue this conversation with the Junior Warden, the Worshipful Master has now moved on to other Brothers and allowed them to begin addressing the Lodge. As more and more Brothers become engaged in the debate, more and more physical and metaphorical light will be born in that room, gradually overcoming the darkness that previously surrounded the Lodge.

Let there be light.

Selected Bibliography

Accuosti, Tom. *The Tao of Masonry* (blog). www.masonictao.com.

Anderson, James. The Constitutions of the Freemasons Containing the History, Charges, Regulations of That Most Ancient and Right Worshipful Fraternity. London: William Hunter, 1723.

Baer, Bob. *Freemasonry in the Bakken*. Podcast. www.bakkenmasons.com.

Baigent, Michael. *Holy Blood, Holy Grail*. New York: Delacorte, 1982.

Brown, Dan. *The Lost Symbol: A Novel*. New York: Doubleday, 2009.

Bullock, Steven C. Revolutionary Brotherhood: Freemasonry and the Transformation of the American Social Order 1730–1840. Chapel Hill: University of North Carolina Press, 1996.

Davis, Robert G. "An Apologia on the Traditions of Freemasonry." *Laudable Pursuit*, February 6, 2015.

Davis, Robert G. "Which Public Image Do We Claim?" *Laudable Pursuit*, June 15, 2015.

Dewan, Shaila, and Robbie Brown. "Black Member Tests Message of Masons in Georgia Lodges," *New York Times*, July 2, 2009.

Eyer, Shawn. "Writing a Masonic Paper." *Philalethes*, vol. 63, 2010.

Fisk, Robert. *Pity the Nation: The Abduction of Lebanon*. New York: Atheneum, 1990.

Grand Lodge of Free and Accepted Masons of the State of New York. "Past Grand Masters." nymasons.org/2015/past-grand-masters/

Hammer, Andrew. The Pursuit of Excellence in Masonic Labour and Observance. Alexandria, VA: Mindhive, 2011.

Harb, Imad. "Lebanon's Confessionalism: Problems and Prospects." United States Institute for Peace, March 30, 2006.

Hauder, Thomas. Socrates Café, Grand Lodge of Iowa. http://grandlodgeofiowa.org/docs/GeneralMasonicEducation/Intro toSocratesCafe.pdf.

Haywood, H.L. "How Operative Masonry Changed to Speculative Masonry: The Period of Transition." *The Builders Magazine*, February 1924.

Hodapp, Christopher. *Freemasons for Dummies*. Hoboken, NJ: Wiley Publishing, 2005.

Johnson, Nick. *The Millennial Freemason* (blog). http://www.millennialfreemason.com.

Marshall, Jason. "Intentional Freemasonry." *Laudable Pursuit*, February 13, 2015.

McConnaughey, Janet. "Ceremony Reflects on Unique Civil War Truce." *The Advocate*, June 9, 2013.

Newton, Joseph Fort. *The Builders*. New York, NY: The Torch Press, 1914.

Packer, George. "The Decade Nobody Knows." *New York Times*. June 10, 2001.

Poll, Michael. "The Masonic Lodge Experience." New Orleans Scottish Rite. YouTube Channel, February 25, 2015.

Putnam, Robert D., and David E. Campbell. *American Grace: How Religion Divides and Unites Us*. New York: Simon & Schuster, 2012.

Rainer, Thom S., and Jess W. Rainer. *The Millennials: Connecting to America's Largest Generation*. Nashville, TN: B&H Pub. Group, 2011.

Rawlinson, George. *Phoenicia: History of a Civilization*. London: I.B. Tauris, 2005.

Richards, Jason. *The 2-Foot Ruler* (blog). https://2footruler.wordpress.com/

Santos, Cory. "When Lincoln Cathedral Was the Tallest Building in the World." *The Lincolnite*, November 6, 2013.

Solomon, Micah. "2015 Is the Year of the Millennial Customer." *Forbes*, December 29, 2014.

Sommer, Dorothe. Freemasonry in the Ottoman Empire: A History of the Fraternity and Its Influence in Syria and the Levant. London: I.B. Tauris, 2015.

Taylor, Paul. The Next America: Boomers, Millennials, and the Looming Generational Showdown. New York: PublicAffairs, 2014.

Times-Picayune (New Orleans). "Yankee Grave Dixie Decorates." October 24, 1937.

Wallace, Ben. "The Masonian Podcast Series." 357 Productions. http://www.357productions.net.

Notes

Introduction

1) Thomas Savini, "Research Inquiry, Message to the Author," Chancellor Robert R. Livingston Masonic Library of NYS Grand Lodge, December 8, 2014, e-mail. The genealogical information regarding my grandfather and father's Masonic career was deduced using the meticulous records that have been held at the library.

2) Sam Friedman, *Millennial Mason Survey*, November 25, 2014. This original survey was created by the author and asked a series of questions of millennial Masons across the country. The survey collected over seventy responses from over twenty-five jurisdictions around the world. The information and quotes in this section are taken directly from this survey. The survey itself is anonymous and therefore there is no way to cite the original authors of these quotes. Login information to the survey will be provided upon request.

3) "Home," Masonic Restoration Foundation,www.masonicrestorationfoundation.org/

4) Robert Herd, "Darkness to Light with Robert Herd," interview by Ben Wallace, video blog post, 357 Productions, June 14, 2014.

5) Christopher Hodapp, *Freemasons for Dummies* (Hoboken, NJ: Wiley Publishing, 2005), 277.

6) Franklin Roosevelt, speech to Architect Lodge, November 7, 1935. This speech was given at the raising of Franklin's two sons, Franklin Jr. and James. The speech can be found in its

entirety at the Franklin D. Roosevelt Presidential Library and Museum Collections.

7) George Washington, Washington's Masonic Correspondence as Found among the Washington Papers in the Library of Congress (Philadelphia: Committee on Library of the Grand Lodge of Pennsylvania, 1915).

8) Christopher Hodapp, *Freemasons for Dummies* (Hoboken, NJ: Wiley Publishing, 2005), 277.

9) Richard Kidwell, "Freemasonry: The Sleeping Giant," *Masonic Service Association Short Talk Bulletin*, 1982.

10) Steven C. Bullock, Revolutionary Brotherhood: Freemasonry and the Transformation of the American Social Order, 1730–1840, (Chapel Hill: University of North Carolina Press, 1996), 318.

11) Joseph Fort Newton, *The Builders*, First Printing, (The Torch Press, New York, 1914), 248.

12) Robert G. Davis, "Which Public Image Do We Claim?" *Laudable Pursuit*, June 15, 2015.

13) Robert G. Davis, "An Apologia on the Traditions of Freemasonry," *Laudable Pursuit*, February 6, 2015.

14) William Grimshaw, *Official History of Freemasonry among the Colored People in North America* (New York: Broadway Publishing Company, 1903), 5–6, 29–30.

Whence Came You

15) Thomas Jefferson, Adams–Jefferson Letters, Monticello, August 1, 1816, 483–85.

16) 1 Kings 7:13, 7:22, (New International Version).

17) David Murray Lyon, History of the Lodge of Edinburgh

(Mary's Chapel) No. 1. Embracing an Account of the Rise and Progress of Freemasonry in Scotland. Edinburgh (William Blackwood and Sons, 1873).

18) James Anderson, The Constitutions of the Freemasons Containing the History, Charges, Regulations of That Most Ancient and Right Worshipful Fraternity (London: William Hunter, 1723), 49.

19) Ibid., 50.

20) Steven C. Bullock, Revolutionary Brotherhood: Freemasonry and the Transformation of the American Social Order, 1730–1840, (Chapel Hill: University of North Carolina Press, 1996), 114.

21) Ibid., 123.

22) Ibid., 129.

23) Ibid., 138.

24) Ibid., 556–57.

25) Albert Pike, "Allocution of the Grand Commander of the Supreme Council of the 33rd Degree for the Southern Jurisdiction of the United States of America," 1884.

26) Masonic Service Association of North America, http://www.msana.com/msastats.asp.

27) Masonic Service Association of North America, http://www.msana.com/msastats.asp. In 1950 there were 3,644,634 Masons in the United States. By 1957, there were 4,085,676 Masons.

28) Robert Gollmar, "Let's Look at the Future," *Philalethes Magazine*, June 1959.

29) Robert Putnam, *American Grace: How Religion Divides and Unites Us* (New York: Simon & Schuster, 2010), 91.

30) Ibid., 92.

Traditional Observance Movement

31) Dan Brown, "Address to London Freemasons," Freemasons Hall, London, May 22 2013, *The Independent Newspaper.* http://www.independent.co.uk/arts-entertainment/books/news/the-freemasons-code-dan-brown-reveals-the-message-that-told-him-the-door-to-the-lodge-is-open-8625968.html

32) Dan Brown, *The Lost Symbol: A Novel* (New York: Doubleday, 2009), 615.

33) Dave Upham, Secretary, Demographic Information from ERAC Lodge #163, n.d., raw data, ERAC Lodge #163, Rochester, NY.

34) Jason Marshall, "Intentional Freemasonry" *Laudable Pursuit,* 13 Feb 2015, http://www.thelaudablepursuit.com/articles/2015/2/13/intentional-freemasonry

Portrait of a Generation

35) Richard Fry, "This Year, Millennials Will Overtake Baby Boomers," Pew Research Center, January 16, 2015.

36) Thom Rainer, *The Millennials: Connecting to America's Largest Generation* (Nashville, TN: B&H Publishing Group, 2011), 18.

37) Ibid., 33.

38) Grlmm, "Re: What do Young Masons Want?" *Reddit,* October 2014.

39) Fitzgeraldb, "Re: What do Young Masons Want?" *Reddit,* September 25, 2014.

40) "Millennials in Adulthood: Detached from Institutions, Networked with Friends," Pew Research Center, 2014.

41) "America's Changing Religious Landscape," Pew Research Center, 2015.

42) "Changing Attitudes on Gay Marriage," Pew Research Center, 2015.

43) The Council of Economic Advisors, "15 Economic Facts about Millennials," Executive Office of the President of the United States, October 2014.

44) Ibid., 11.

45) Jmstallard, "Re: Millennial / Young Masons, What Do You / We Want?" *Reddit*, February 25, 2015.

46) Sam Friedman, *Millennial Mason Survey*, November 25, 2014.

47) Michah Solomon, "2015 Is the Year of the Millennial Customer," *Forbes*, December 29, 2014.

48) Thom Rainer, *The Millennials: Connecting to America's Largest Generation* (Nashville, TN: B&H Publishing Group, 2011), 47.

49) Ibid., 269.

50) Michael Lipka, "Millennials Increasingly Are Driving Growth of 'Nones,'" Pew Research Center, May 12, 2015.

51) "Religion among the Millennials," Pew Research Center, February 17, 2010.

52) Thom Rainer, *The Millennials: Connecting to America's Largest Generation* (Nashville, TN: B&H Publishing Group, 2011), 243.

53) Ibid., 47.

54) Poor_and_Blind, "Re: What Do Young Masons Want?" *Reddit*, September 2014.

55) Thom Rainer, *The Millennials: Connecting to America's Largest Generation* (Nashville, TN: B&H Publishing Group, 2011), 117.

56) Bobbie Couch, "Stop Calling Millennials Selfish, 87% of Millennials Donated To Charity Last Year: Report," *Huffington*

Post, June 19, 2014.

57) Sam Friedman, Millennial Mason Survey, November 25, 2014.

Men of Tyre

58) Claudia Roth Pierpont, "Found in Translation: The Modern Arabic Novel," *The New Yorker,* January 18, 2010.

59) Tom Perry, "Factbox: Facts on Lebanon's Economy," *Reuters,* June 8, 2009.

60) Dorothe Sommer, Freemasonry in the Ottoman Empire: A History of the Fraternity and Its Influence in Syria and the Levant (London: I.B Tauris, 2015), 8.

61) Ibid., 29.

62) Ibid., 193.

63) Ibid., 7.

Millennial Lodge #1

64) Andrew Hammer, *Observing the Craft: The Pursuit of Excellence in Masonic Labour and Observance* (Alexandria, VA: Mindhive Publishing, 2010). This quote is originally taken from the 1963 proceedings of the Grand Lodge of West Virginia, but since I originally encountered them in Andrew Hammer's work, I chose to cite him instead of the primary source.

65) Joseph Salem, "Freemasonry and World Peace," *The Israeli Freemason,*
http://www.mastermason.com/fmisrael/peace.html. I was not able to find the original publication of the Israeli Freemason.

66) Thomas   Hauder,   Socrates   Café.   July   1,   2009,

http://grandlodgeofiowa.org/docs/GeneralMasonicEducatio
n/IntrotoSocratesCafe.pdf.

67) John Patrick, Dogma: The Deconstruction and Evolution of
Our Psyche, (Xlibris, 2013), 55.

Made in the USA
San Bernardino, CA
26 December 2015